SPEIGHT'S
SOUTHERN MAN
COOKBOOK

✳ ✳ ✳

The founders of Speight's Brewery 1876: James Speight,
Charles Greenslade and William Dawson

SPEIGHT'S
SOUTHERN MAN
COOKBOOK

✳ ✳ ✳

GENEROUS TO A FAULT

RANDOM HOUSE
NEW ZEALAND

A RANDOM HOUSE BOOK published by Random House New Zealand
18 Poland Road, Glenfield, Auckland, New Zealand

For more information about our titles go to www.randomhouse.co.nz

Random House New Zealand is part of the Random House Group
New York   London   Sydney   Auckland   Delhi   Johannesburg

A catalogue record for this book is available from the National
Library of New Zealand

First published 2010

ISBN 978 1 86979 395 1

Design: Gary Stewart, The Gas Project
Writing: Nicola McCloy
Photography: Aaron McLean
Food styling: Fiona Smith
Props: Tamara West

Printed in China by Everbest Printing Co Ltd

www.drinkresponsibly.co.nz™

CONTENTS

Macraes Road on the way to Macraes Flat, Central Otago

SOUNDS LIKE SHE'S
LEFT YOU WITH THE
SHORT END OF THE
STICK?

NO, NO, SHARP END
OF THE BUILDING.

INTRODUCTION

Over its long and proud history, Speight's has produced award-winning traditional ales and beers using fine ingredients and pure water from New Zealand.

In 1876 James Speight, Charles Greenslade and William Dawson set up Speight's Brewery in Dunedin. Still on the same Rattray Street site it has occupied ever since, Speight's Brewery has become one of Dunedin and Otago's biggest icons – no longer just the 'Pride of the South', the Speight's brand is now one of New Zealand's most loved beers.

The Speight's Ale Houses have become an intrinsic part of the history of Speight's. Found within the historic brewery is the original ale house, which opened in 1999. All the superb tap ales served at The Speight's Ale House are brewed right there on site, just as they have been since 1876. The success of the original led to the establishment of an extensive network of ale houses throughout the country, most recently The Gables Speight's Ale House in Auckland's Jervois Rd.

When the original ale house was opened, the challenge given to the chefs was to produce hearty, value-for-money servings of Southern fare. This is still the case, with today's menus still featuring Speight's Ale House classics like seafood chowder, blue cod, lamb shanks, steak, and venison, as well as vegetarian options. All meals are expertly matched to one of the fine tap ales available, creating authentic Southern dining experiences all the way throughout the country.

Speight's may have originated from rural South Island, but is increasingly popular in the North Island too. The Speight's Ale Houses mean any Kiwi can enjoy traditional Southern grub washed down with a Speight's, but the fare remains true to its Southern values: generosity of spirit, mateship and 'can-do' attitude.

The Speight's Ale Houses have developed a great reputation as the place to go for generous portions of hearty southern fare, matched with Speight's beers and some good old-fashioned Southern hospitality. That's why we decided to take the concept one step further and develop this cookbook. In it you'll find favourite recipes taken from our Speight's Ale Houses, so you can bring the Southern hospitality home to share with your friends and family. There's nothing difficult or exotic about this food – it's just hearty, delicious, quality tucker – with a few beer recommendations along the way.

I hope this cookbook is one you'll keep turning to time and time again when you want to experience the Speight's Southern Man legend at home.

Peter Kean
Managing Director
Lion Nathan

ALE HOUSES

AUCKLAND
Cardrona Speight's Ale
House
37 Normanby Road
Mt Eden

The Gables Speight's Ale
House
248 Jervois Road
(cnr Jervois Road &
Kelmarna Ave)
Herne Bay

HAMILTON
Speight's Ale House
Hamilton
30 Liverpool Street

NAPIER
Speight's Ale House Napier
80 West Quay
Ahuriri

PALMERSTON NORTH
Speight's Ale House
Palmerston North
27 Grey Street

WELLINGTON
Shepherd's Arms
285 Tinakori Road
Thorndon

Speight's Ale House Petone
75–81 Jackson Street
Petone

GREYMOUTH
Speight's Ale House
Greymouth
130 Mawhera Quay

CHRISTCHURCH
Speight's Ale House Bealey
263 Bealey Avenue

Speight's Ale House Tower
Junction
55 Clarence Street
Riccarton

Speight's Ale House
Ferrymead
2A Water Place
Ferrymead

ASHBURTON
Speight's Ale House
Ashburton
245 Burnett Street

TIMARU
Speight's Ale House Timaru
2 George Street

DUNEDIN
Speight's Ale House
Dunedin
200 Rattray Street

QUEENSTOWN
Speight's Ale House
Queenstown
Cnr Stanley & Ballarat
Streets

INVERCARGILL
Speight's Ale House
Invercargill
38 Dee Street

Auckland

Hamilton

Napier

Palmerston North

Wellington

Greymouth

Christchurch

Ashburton

Timaru

Queenstown

Dunedin

Invercargill

Mt Ida Range, Central Otago

LIGHT MEALS

METHOD	SERVES	MEAT	TIME
SIMMER	4	**SEAFOOD**	**50 MINUTES**

SEAFOOD CHOWDER

A rib-sticking bowl of seafood chowder always tastes best if you've gone out and got the ingredients yourself – and we're not talking supermarkets.

30 g butter
1 large onion, finely chopped
50 ml white wine
1 large potato, peeled and cut into about
    2.5 cm chunks
1 litre fish stock
salt and freshly ground black pepper
12 fresh mussels in their shell, cleaned
    and de-bearded

250 g firm white fish fillets, such as blue
    cod, snapper, or hapuka/groper, cut
    into about 2 cm chunks
150 g prawn meat
12 scallops
100 ml cream
2 teaspoons finely chopped fennel or dill
    leaves

Method
Melt the butter in a large saucepan and add the onion. Cook over a low heat until soft, about 10 minutes.

Add the white wine and reduce by half, then add the potato and fish stock. Season well with salt and freshly ground black pepper. Bring to the boil, then reduce heat, cover and simmer for about 20 minutes or until the potato is soft.

Remove from the heat, allow to cool a little, then purée in a blender or food processor until smooth.

Return liquid to rinsed-out saucepan.

Place mussels in a saucepan with 1 cm water, cover, and cook on a high heat until they open. (Throw away any that don't open.)

Bring the liquid back to the boil and add the fish, prawns and scallops. Cook for 3 minutes or until the seafood is just cooked, it will keep on cooking in the hot liquid.

Remove from the heat and stir in the cream and fennel or dill.

Place 3 mussels in each of 4 warmed soup bowls and ladle chowder over, dividing the seafood as evenly as possible.

Serve with fresh bread.

Tip: For extra flavour add 1 sliced fennel bulb in with the onion. The green fennel fronds or tops can be chopped and added at the end of cooking.

METHOD	SERVES	MEAT	TIME
SIMMER	6	**CHICKEN STOCK**	**40 MINUTES**

HEARTY PUMPKIN SOUP

There's nothing better than a piping hot bowl of soup after an early morning lambing beat or a long day out mustering.

1 kg pumpkin, peeled and cut into
  even-sized chunks
1 onion, peeled and cut into quarters
3 cloves garlic, peeled
3 cm piece fresh ginger, peeled and
  roughly chopped
2 sprigs thyme
2 bay leaves

1 tablespoon olive oil
¼ cup white wine
1 litre chicken stock
½ teaspoon cumin
¼ teaspoon cinnamon
¼ teaspoon nutmeg
salt and freshly ground black pepper

Method
Preheat the oven to 180°C.

Place pumpkin, onion, garlic, ginger, thyme and bay leaves into a roasting tray. Toss with olive oil and roast 20–30 minutes until pumpkin is tender.

Once cooked, remove the thyme and bay leaves and discard. Transfer the rest to a large saucepan.

Place roasting tray on the heat and deglaze with wine, removing any bits in the tray. Add to the pumpkin mix.

Add chicken stock, cumin, cinnamon and nutmeg. Stir and bring to a simmer. Simmer covered for 5 minutes. Cool a little, then purée in a blender or food processor until smooth.

Season with salt and freshly ground black pepper and add more stock if soup is too thick.

METHOD	SERVES	MEAT	TIME
SIMMER	4	**ONLY IN THE STOCK**	**45 MINUTES**

KUMARA AND BEETROOT SOUP

Say 'borscht' to a Southern Man and he's likely to reply 'Bless you, mate!' But he's bound to love this Kiwi twist on a classic Russian beetroot soup.

1 large kumara, peeled and cut into even-sized chunks
1 large beetroot, peeled and cut into even-sized chunks
1 onion, peeled, and cut into even-sized chunks
1 tablespoon red wine vinegar or malt vinegar

1.5 litres chicken or vegetable stock
juice of half a lemon
salt and freshly ground black pepper
4 dessertspoons sour cream, to serve
about 12 chives, to serve

Method

In a large saucepan put the vegetables, vinegar, stock and ½ teaspoon freshly ground black pepper. Bring to the boil, then simmer for 30–35 minutes until beetroot is tender.

Cool a little then purée in a blender or food processor until smooth, adding extra stock if too thick.

Add lemon juice and season to taste with salt and freshly ground black pepper.

Serve with sour cream and snipped chives.

Tip: Choose vegetables of a similar size.

METHOD	SERVES	MEAT	TIME
GRILL	4	**NONE**	**20 MINUTES**

CHEESE ROLLS

Cheese roll recipes are usually a well kept family secret down south. We had to twist some arms to get the Ale Houses in Petone and Napier to give you theirs. These are great on a cold winter's day with a bowl of your favourite soup.

Speight's Ale House, Petone

2 cups grated tasty cheddar cheese
1 x 250 ml can reduced cream
1 packet onion soup mix (32 g)
1 loaf toast bread, or 16 slices
100 g butter, melted

Method
Preheat the grill to high.

In a bowl, combine the cheese, reduced cream and onion soup mix.

Cut the crusts off the bread slices and use a rolling pin to flatten each slice a little.

Spread cheese mixture evenly over the bread slices and roll up into a cigar shape.

Brush each roll evenly with melted butter and place in a shallow baking tray.

Place under the grill and grill until golden brown, turning to ensure all sides are cooked.

Makes about 16 rolls.

Speight's Ale House, Napier

1–2 eggs, lightly beaten
2 cups grated tasty cheddar cheese
1 onion, finely chopped
salt and freshly ground black pepper
1 loaf toast bread or 16 slices
100 g butter, melted

Method
Preheat the grill to high.

In a bowl, combine the eggs, cheese and onion. Season well with salt and freshly ground black pepper.

Cut the crusts off the bread slices and use a rolling pin to flatten each slice a little.

Spread cheese mixture evenly over the bread slices and roll up into a cigar shape.

Brush each roll evenly with melted butter and place in a shallow baking tray.

Place under the grill and grill until golden brown, turning to ensure all sides are cooked.

Makes about 16 rolls.

METHOD	SERVES	MEAT	TIME
BAKE	8	NONE	25 MINUTES

THE OLD MASTER'S CHEESE SCONES

The Old Master serves his scones with soup. He reckons they'll help keep the flu away in the tough winter months with the cayenne pepper giving you a good kick just when you need it.

2 cups flour
2 teaspoons baking powder
½ teaspoon salt
⅓ teaspoon cayenne pepper

50 g butter
¾ cup grated cheddar cheese
¾ cup milk

Method
Preheat the oven to 200°C.
    Into a mixing bowl, sift the flour, baking powder, salt and cayenne pepper.
    Add the butter, cut into small pieces.
    Blend the butter into the flour mixture with your fingertips until the mixture resembles coarse breadcrumbs.
    With a table knife, stir in the cheese and milk to form a soft dough.
    Using your hands, form the dough into the shape of a cob loaf and cut into 8 pieces. Form each piece into a half-inch thick square. Place the squares of dough, spaced well apart, on a baking sheet.
    Bake for 12–15 minutes or until they have risen and are golden brown.
    Serve immediately.

Speight's Brewery, Rattray Street, Dunedin, 1889

TIMELINE

James Speight,
mid 1880s

William Dawson,
mid 1880s

Charles Greenslade,
mid 1880s

1876
James Speight, Charles Greenslade and William Dawson resign from Well Park Brewery to establish their own brewery in Dunedin's Rattray Street. The trio's first brew was Speight's Ale, which was made on 4 April. On 6 June, they got their brewers' licence.

1880
Speight's wins two gold medals at the Melbourne Exhibition. Back in Dunedin, a new brewhouse is built.

1887
Speight's becomes the biggest brewery in the country, exporting to Australia, Fiji and Tahiti. A sombre mood comes over the brewery as its founder and namesake, James Speight, passes away on 16 August. Another of the company's founders, William Dawson, becomes mayor of Dunedin later in the year.

1890
William Dawson elected to parliament as member for Dunedin Suburbs.

1897
Speight's becomes a limited liability company with directors, Charles Greenslade, William Dawson and James Speight's son Charles. Hugh Adam is appointed company secretary.

1902
The Speight's name is registered as a trademark. The Shamrock Hotel, site of the current Dunedin Alehouse, is closed down by its owners – the Presbyterian Church – and reopens as an auction house.

Everything before 1876 is known as BS – Before Speight's.

1876

1902

1879
A beer competition is held at Sydney International Exhibition. Speight's Strong Ale is highly commended.

1882
Speight's wins two gold medals at the Christchurch International Exhibition.

1884
A new malthouse is opened on land leased from the Presbyterian Church.

1889
New Zealand and South Seas Exhibition held in Dunedin. Speight's wins three gold medals. The brewhouse is substantially rebuilt.

1893
The Alcoholic Liquor Control Bill is passed seeing the number of pubs granted licences slashed. To counter the growing prohibition movement, Speight's publish a booklet called 'The History of a Glass of Beer' outlining the positive aspects of the brewing industry.

1898
The brewery expands with a new building across Rattray Street. The spring under the brewery is tapped.

1908
Ernest Shackleton takes casks of Speight's to Antarctica on board the *Nimrod*. Speight's acquires another Dunedin brewery, Strachan's.

1917
Drinking age raised from 16 to 20. Six o'clock closing introduced. Another of Speight's founders, Charles Greenslade, passes away on 19 October. His son Bob sees the Greenslade name remain on the company's board.

1922
Along with other Dunedin businesses, Speight's starts their own shipping company and the *Holmdale* is pressed into service sailing beer to the thirsty north. The ship becomes known as 'The Mercy Ship'.

1925
Charles Speight takes a leading role in the staging of the New Zealand and South Seas Exhibition. Lake Logan is reclaimed to create Logan Park, the site of the exhibition.

1935
Bob Greenslade passes away on 16 June 1935. Hugh Adam, formerly Speight's company secretary, succeeds him as New Zealand Breweries director.

1940
On 25 June a huge fire destroys the malthouse and cellar buildings on the southwest side of Rattray Street. A week later Hugh Adams passes away. Hugh Speight takes over as brewery manager. Construction of the new brewery is completed.

1917

1940

1904
The brewery expands again with a new malthouse built.

1913
Norah McGhie becomes Speight's first full-time female employee. Speight's buys its first motorised truck for delivering casks to local pubs.

1919
Garage built for Speight's motor vehicles.

1923
The threat of prohibition sees Speight's and nine smaller breweries from around the country amalgamate to become New Zealand Breweries Ltd. Charles Speight and Bob Greenslade are appointed directors. The third of Speight's founders, William Dawson passes away on 23 July.

1928
On 19 February, Charles Speight passes away, aged 61. His funeral is one of the largest ever seen in Dunedin. His son Hugh succeeds him as a director of New Zealand Breweries.

1937
Work on a new brewery building starts. One of its most distinctive features is the barrel at the top of its chimney, which is still a landmark on Dunedin's skyline today. The barrel is thought to have been a draughtsman's joke that Hugh Speight took a liking to.

Charles Speight and Bob Greenslade, c. 1900

TIMELINE

JUST RIGHT!

. . . LIGHT, BRIGHT, GOLDEN ALE OF EXQUISITE FLAVOUR!

SPEIGHTS ALE

1942
The cellar is converted into an air raid shelter in case of aerial bombing of the city. Government legislate for a reduction in the strength of beer causing Speight's to drop their slogan, 'Purity, Body and Strength'.

1955
Speight's first lager, Pilsener is launched.

1961
Speight's start producing a 'near beer' called Tom Thumb, primarily for sale at Forbury Trotting Club's night meets, where six o'clock closing meant full strength beer could not be sold. While it remained on sale until 1967, it wasn't the brewery's best work.

1976
Speight's celebrates its centennial by donating $10,000 to Dunedin Public Library and putting out a special centennial brew.

1980
Speight's staff compete to come up with a new slogan for the company. First place was Jackie Peperkoorn's 'Follow the stars'. In second was Malcolm Campbell's 'Pride of the South'.

1984
Speight's in cans first come onto the market. The beer was sent to Christchurch by train and canned there.

1942   1984

1946
New kauri fermenting gyles are brought into service, four of which remain in use in 2010.

1951
The first tanker delivery of Speight's is made to the Criterion Hotel.

1960
Possibly the darkest time in the history of Speight's. New Zealand Breweries decide to streamline their beer production and rebrand all local beers with the same name – Lucky Beer. For the first time since 1876, there is no Speight's. Thankfully, customer resistance was so strong the rebranding only lasted two months and Speight's was back and Lucky disappeared.

1969
Hugh Speight passes away aged 64. Before his death, he put in place plans for a new bottling plant, which opened the following year.

1977
Speight's undertakes the first of many sporting sponsorships with Dunedin's senior grade rugby competition becoming the Speight's Championship. New Zealand Breweries' name is changed to Lion Breweries.

1981
The first Coast to Coast is completed.

1983
The first Speight's brewery tours take place.

FERMENTING GYLE No3

1991
Speight's donates $250,000 for the refurbishment of Carisbrook. The cheque was delivered to the ground attached to the leg of future All Black Arran Pene as he parachuted into Carisbrook. Arran now runs Speight's Hamilton Ale House. Otago rugby repay Speight's by winning the national championship.

1993
Speight's Gold Medal Ale wins first prize in the open draught section of the Australian Beer Awards.

1994
Speight's Distinction Ale is launched to mark the company's 118th birthday.

1999
The first Speight's Ale House is opened in Dunedin, by Prime Minister Jenny Shipley.

2001
Speight's 125th anniversary.

2007
The Great Beer Delivery takes place from Dunedin to London.

2010
Speight's launches new Central Otago packaging and new longer neck bottle.

1991   2007   2010

1992
The Speight's stand at Carisbrook is opened. Speight's Old Dark is launched.

1996
The Super 12 is launched with Speight's sponsoring the Otago Highlanders.

1998
Speight's is sold in London for the first time through the Australian chain of Walkabout pubs.

2000
The Southern Man statue at Dunedin Airport is gifted to the city by Speight's to mark the millennium.

2006
Speight's Distinction Ale wins Best in Class in the dark beer class at the International Beer Awards. The Otago rugby team becomes Speight's Otago.

2008
Summit lager is launched.

2009
Traverse lager is launched. Distinction wins Best in Class for International-style Lager at New Zealand Beer Awards.

1987
The Southern Man advertising campaign is born.

METHOD	SERVES	MEAT	TIME
FRY	6	**CHICKEN LIVER**	**30 MINUTES**

BEALEY'S SPEIGHT'S PÂTÉ

Down at Speight's Ale House Bealey, in Christchurch,
they know how to do great things with chicken livers . . .
among other things.

100 g butter
½ onion, finely chopped
1 small carrot, peeled and sliced
1 small stick celery, lightly peeled to
    remove any stringy bits, sliced
125 g button mushrooms, cleaned
1 sprig thyme
1 bay leaf

½ tablespoon wholegrain mustard
200 ml cream
250 g chicken livers, trimmed of fatty
    pieces and greenish stained liver
salt and freshly ground black pepper
6 tablespoons clarified butter
fresh bay leaves or whole peppercorns

Method
Melt 50 g of the butter in a large frying pan and cook the vegetables and herbs until
soft, about 10 minutes.

Add the mustard and cream, bring to the boil and simmer until thick, about 3
minutes. Remove herbs and transfer vegetables to a bowl.

Melt the remaining 50 g of butter in the frying pan. Over a high heat, cook the
chicken livers quickly on both sides until golden brown but still soft in the middle.

Return vegetable mixture to the frying pan, mix well and season with salt and
freshly ground black pepper.

Blend thoroughly in a food processor or put through a food mill.

Spoon into 6 small bowls and spoon clarified butter over. Place 2–3 fresh bay
leaves or a few whole peppercorns on top.

Cover with plastic wrap and chill well.

Serve with toasted slices of Ale House Loaf (see page 232).

Tip: The surface of chicken liver pâté will oxidise, so it is best to cover it with a thin
layer of clarified butter. To make clarified butter, melt butter until the solids fall to
the bottom of the saucepan. Spoon or ladle off the liquid butter.

METHOD	SERVES	MEAT	TIME
NONE	2	PÂTÉ	5 MINUTES

PLOUGHMAN'S PLATTER

If you've got a Southern Man coming round for dinner, chances are he'll arrive hungry. This selection of tasty stuff should keep his laughing gear occupied until dinner.

1 x Ale House Loaf, sliced, and toasted if
    wished (see page 232)
125 g solid wedge of brie
4–6 slices salami
1 small pot chicken liver pâté
(see page 31)

1 small pot hummus (see page 235)
1 small pot beetroot relish (see page 235)
12 small gherkins or 6 large gherkins

METHOD	SERVES	MEAT	TIME
FRY	4	**NONE**	**30 MINUTES**

GOLDEN FRITTERS

These golden corn fritters are the perfect breakfast to set
you up for a hard day's work, or a hard day's fishing, or
a hard day's watching rugby.

15 g butter, plus extra for cooking
    fritters
1 small red onion, finely chopped
1 clove garlic, crushed
2 eggs
50 ml milk

3 heaped tablespoons self-raising flour
1 x 300 g can whole kernel corn,
    drained
1 x 300 g can creamed corn
1 tablespoon chopped coriander
salt and freshly ground black pepper

Method
Melt butter in a frying pan, add the onion and garlic, and cook gently until soft,
about 5 minutes.

In a large bowl lightly whisk the eggs and milk together. Sift the flour on top
and whisk until there are no lumps.

Stir in the corn, coriander, softened onion and garlic and season with salt and
black pepper.

Add a knob of butter to the frying pan. In batches, drop in large tablespoonfuls
of the fritter mixture and cook on both sides until golden, about 4 minutes.

Serve hot with a tomato and coriander salsa (see page 238).

Makes about 12 fritters.

METHOD	SERVES	MEAT	TIME
FRY	4	**WHITEBAIT**	**30 MINUTES**

WEST COAST WHITEBAIT PATTIES

Who better to give you their secret whitebait pattie recipe than the good blokes at the Speight's Ale House in Greymouth.

Croutons
1 x day-old breadstick, sliced
olive oil

1 clove garlic

Method
Brush breadstick slices with oil and grill until golden. Swipe each slice with a cut garlic clove while warm.

Garlic butter sauce
1 tablespoon white wine vinegar
1 egg
1 egg yolk

1 clove garlic, crushed
200 g butter
salt

Method
In a small saucepan, heat the vinegar. Place the egg, egg yolk and garlic in a small blender, pour on the hot vinegar and blend.

Melt the butter and while still hot, and with the motor running, drizzle down the feeder tube onto the egg mixture. Season with salt and set aside. (Alternatively, make the butter sauce in a double boiler – a bowl over a saucepan of just-boiling water.)
Tip: The butter sauce can be made ahead and kept warm in a small soup Thermos.

Whitebait patties
5 eggs
500 g West Coast whitebait
pinch of salt

juice of 1 lemon
knob of butter for frying
2 lemons for wedges

Method
Lightly beat the eggs with a fork. Add the whitebait, pinch of salt and lemon juice.

Heat the butter in a large frying pan over a medium heat and fry mixture in batches for about 2 minutes, turning once.

Serve whitebait patties with the garlic butter sauce, croutons and plenty of lemon wedges.

METHOD	SERVES	MEAT	TIME
GRILL	4	**OYSTERS**	**8 MINUTES**

SHUCK 'EM

Your average Southern Man can't wait for 1 March and the opening of the Bluff oyster season. Not that they need oysters, mind. They just like them – a lot. Of course oysters are superb served raw, straight from the shell. However, if you must cook 'em, this recipe will do the trick. It's a classic Oysters Kilpatrick.

24 fresh oysters, in their shells
rock salt
1 tablespoon Worcestershire sauce
60 g butter

4 rashers streaky bacon, finely chopped
salt and freshly ground black pepper
2 tablespoons chopped parsley, to serve
lemon wedges, to serve

Method
Preheat the grill to high.
    Arrange the oysters on a bed of rock salt in a large shallow ovenproof dish.
    Combine the Worcestershire sauce and butter in a small saucepan and heat the butter until it melts and the mixture begins to bubble around the edges of the saucepan. Remove from the heat.
    Spoon a little of the Worcestershire sauce and butter mixture over each oyster then top evenly with the diced bacon. Season with salt and freshly ground black pepper.
    Cook under the preheated grill for 3–4 minutes until the bacon is crisp.
    Sprinkle with parsley and serve with lemon wedges.

SOUTHERN MAN'S CALENDAR

JAN	FEB	MAR	APR	MAY	JUN
New Year's Day – 1 January				Opening of Bluff oyster season – 1 May	Entries open for next year's Speight's Coast to Coast – 1 June
Central Otago Trotting Club race meeting at Omakau – 3 January	Wellington Sevens – early February		April Fools' Day – 1 April Anniversary of the first brewing of Speight's – 4 April	Duck shooting season – first weekend in May	
James Speight's birthday – 6 January	Go bush to avoid Valentine's Day – 13-15 February Super Rugby begins. Go you Highlanders!!		Leicester Rutledge's birthday – 12 April	Charlie Saxton's birthday – 23 May	Anniversary of James Speight being granted a brewer's licence – 6 June
	Speight's Coast to Coast – second weekend in February	Otago Anniversary Day – celebrated on the Monday closest to the 23rd	Middlemarch Singles' Ball – every second Easter Anzac Day – 25 April	Bluff Oyster Festival – third weekend in May	Queenstown Winter Festival feat. Speight's Dog Derby and Dog Barking – last week of June/first week of July

GOING A LONG WAY FOR A COLD SPEIGHT'S

243km

WE MAKE 'EM TOUGH DOWN HERE
PROUD SPONSOR OF THE HIGHLANDERS

JUL	AUG	SEPT	OCT	NOV	DEC

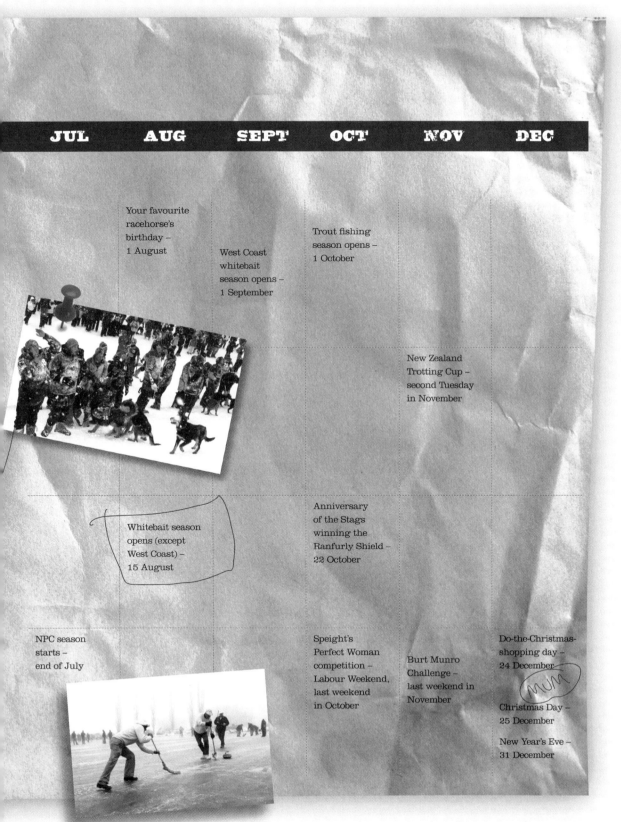

Your favourite racehorse's birthday – 1 August

West Coast whitebait season opens – 1 September

Trout fishing season opens – 1 October

New Zealand Trotting Cup – second Tuesday in November

Whitebait season opens (except West Coast) – 15 August

Anniversary of the Stags winning the Ranfurly Shield – 22 October

NPC season starts – end of July

Speight's Perfect Woman competition – Labour Weekend, last weekend in October

Burt Munro Challenge – last weekend in November

Do-the-Christmas-shopping day – 24 December

MUM

Christmas Day – 25 December

New Year's Eve – 31 December

'CAN YOU SMELL BURNING?'
THE TALE OF MURDOCH MACKENZIE

If you get a job at your favourite brewery it makes sense that you'd stay there for as long as possible, right? That's certainly the case with Speight's. Over the years, a lot of their staff members have spent nearly their entire working lives at the brewery.

No one has yet challenged Jim de Clifford, who started working as a despatch clerk in 1894 and finally retired in 1954 after 60 years' service. If anyone is ever going to outdo de Clifford's record, it is likely to be Don Gordon who has been working for Speight's since 1960. He's in fine company in the 50-years-plus club with Tom Rodger and Robert Greenslade.

The number of staff members who have made it to their fortieth anniversary at the brewery runs well into double figures, but there's one name that stands out in that list. And that's the one and only Murdoch MacKenzie.

With a name like that, Murdoch could only come from one place. Yep, that's right. He was a Scotsman. Unsurprisingly, Murdoch MacKenzie was a bit of a law unto himself. For the whole forty-plus years he worked at Speight's, he did things his way and beggar the consequences . . .

As a cellar foreman, Murdoch MacKenzie worked in, well, the cellar. He loved working for the brewery but he wasn't so keen on being watched by the bosses. When he saw any of the head sherangs approaching, he'd make sure his colleagues knew it, calling out, 'Here comes the boss – scatter yerselves together!'

Down there, in the bowels of the building, smoking was absolutely banned on account of the risk of fire breaking out.

Of course, Murdoch took no notice of this ban and would happily puff away on his pipe. If any of the bosses came along he would quickly hide his pipe under his apron until the coast was clear. One day though, his plan didn't quite go to plan.

Charles Speight was walking past and thought he could smell burning. He asked the doughty cellar foreman if he could smell it too. Pipe safely hidden in his apron, Murdoch MacKenzie sniffed the air and responded in the negative, 'Och, it's probably the biscuit factory next door.' Mr Speight might have believed his story but for the fact that at that precise moment, the Scotsman's shirt burst into flames!

It wasn't just smoking that MacKenzie liked to indulge in down in the cellar. Some nights he'd put in some unpaid, ahem, overtime sampling the brewery's fine product. Unsurprisingly, the dreaded bosses weren't all that keen on having a thirsty Scotsman loose in the brewery so he was told that he had to leave as soon as his day's work was done. Did Murdoch MacKenzie listen? Did he heck.

One night, after a lengthy sampling session, the phone rang and Murdoch somewhat foolishly answered it. Charles Speight was on the other end of the line. It didn't take a long conversation before Mr Speight recognised the thick Scottish accent. 'Is that you Mac? What the hell are you doing there?'

Murdoch thought quickly and decided to pretend that he was another Scotsman who was meant to be working at that time of night. His response, 'Och no, Mr Speight, it's not me. It's Geordie Dickson . . .'

Speight's advertisement, 1930s

SPEIGHT'S COAST TO COAST

In February every year a migration across the South Island takes place. In one weekend, 800 people run, bike and kayak from one side of the island to the other. It's not a religious pilgrimage – it's more serious than that. It's the world's premier multi-sport event: the Speight's Coast to Coast.

Taking either one or two days, individual competitors and two-person teams make the 243 kilometre trek from Kumara Beach on the west coast to Sumner Beach on the east coast. Along the way they cycle 140 kilometres, run 36 kilometres and kayak 67 kilometres. And after that ultimate test of endurance they still have the energy to crack open a well-deserved cold Speight's.

Competitors range from elite athletes to weekend warriors, with top athletes completing the course in as little as 10.5 hours, whereas the slowest time ever recorded was 24.5 hours. Regardless of their level of ability everyone who competes does so alongside their mates – their support crews and their fellow competitors. Often it's only

their mates that make the difference between finishing and quitting.

It's that mateship that has seen Speight's sponsor the race since its early days in 1984. The brewery has been so supportive of the race that they even created a low-carb beer in its honour – Speight's Traverse.

Every year some 800 competitors crack open a cold Speight's having reached the finish line on Sumner Beach. It's a far cry from the first race in 1982, when the event's godfather Robin Judkins sent 77 competitors off on a cross-country odyssey. With Robin at the helm, the event has continued to grow in popularity every year with competitors coming from all over the world to take part.

To everyone involved in the planning and management of the event, to all the support teams, to all the event volunteers and to all the competitors, there's only one thing to be said:

Good on ya, mate!

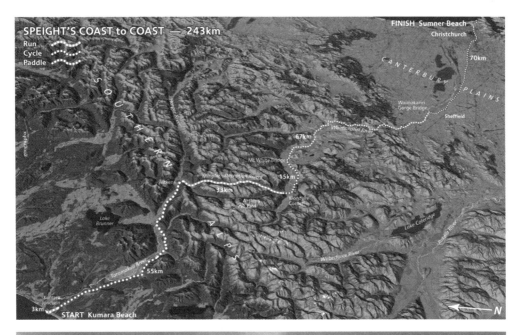

METHOD	SERVES	MEAT	TIME
BAKE	4	**CHICKEN**	**40 MINUTES**

SOUTHERN SALAD

The Southern Man is always a gentleman. If the lady wants salad, the lady gets salad – with chicken and bacon, mind.

Salad
4 chicken breasts, skin on
olive oil for rubbing
salt and freshly ground black pepper
8 rashers streaky bacon
300–350 g cos lettuce
4 soft-boiled eggs (cooked for 7 minutes
    in simmering water)

3 tablespoons chopped parsley, to serve
60 g anchovy fillets, to serve

Croutons
1 x day-old breadstick, sliced
olive oil for brushing
1 clove garlic

Method
Preheat the oven to 190°C.

Rub chicken with olive oil and sprinkle with salt and freshly ground black pepper.

Heat a large frying pan over a medium heat. Place chicken breasts skin-side down and brown for 2 minutes on each side.

Transfer to a roasting dish. Cook in preheated oven for 15 minutes. Remove from oven and allow to cool before shredding into strips.

Turn the oven to grill and heat to high.

Brush breadstick slices with olive oil and grill until golden. Swipe with cut garlic while warm.

Grill bacon until crisp. Drain on kitchen paper.

To serve, divide the cos lettuce between 4 serving plates. Moisten with a little Caesar Salad Dressing (see page 237). Scatter over the chicken and bacon. Place the croutons and halved soft-boiled eggs on top and sprinkle with the chopped parsley and anchovies.

Drizzle over a little more dressing and eat.

METHOD	SERVES	MEAT	TIME
BARBECUE	4	**LAMB**	**40 MINUTES**

CANTERBURY LAMB SALAD

If a Southern Man is going to eat a salad, you'd better be sure there's going to be a bit of meat in there.

600 g butternut pumpkin, peeled, seeds removed, cut into 3 cm chunks
3 tablespoons olive oil
salt and freshly ground black pepper
600 g lamb backstrap, trimmed of all sinew
250 g asparagus, trimmed

1 large red onion, cut into thin wedges, leaving root intact
60 g feta cheese
2 tablespoons pine nuts, toasted
60–80 g or 4 handfuls baby rocket leaves
4 tablespoons of Balsamic Dressing (see page 239)

Method
Preheat the oven to 200°C.

Place the pumpkin into a shallow roasting dish and toss with 1 tablespoon of olive oil and season with salt and freshly ground black pepper. Place in the oven and roast for 20–30 minutes until soft and golden.

With a sharp knife, holding the blade parallel with the bench, slice most of the way through the middle of each piece of lamb. Open out and flatten each piece a little with the flat of your hand.

Preheat a barbecue plate or grill plate until hot. Rub the lamb with 1 tablespoon of oil and some black pepper. Cook for 2 minutes on each side.

Transfer the lamb to a warm plate, season with salt and cover loosely with foil to rest and keep warm.

Lightly toss the asparagus and red onion with the remaining oil and place on the grill. Cook until just tender to the bite.

Place asparagus, red onion and roasted pumpkin on a large serving platter or 4 serving plates.

Slice the lamb into thin slices and place on top of the vegetables.

Crumble the feta cheese over and sprinkle the toasted pine nuts on top.

Place the rocket to the side and drizzle with Balsamic Dressing (see page 239).

Serve immediately.

Tips: You could replace the butternut pumpkin with kumara, carrot, zucchini or capsicum.

To toast pine nuts heat 1 teaspoon oil in a small frying pan and add 1 cup pine nuts. Stir constantly for 2–3 minutes until golden.

METHOD	SERVES	MEAT	TIME
FRY	4	**CHICKEN**	**20 MINUTES**

CHICKEN SALAD

Just a wee bit flash.

600 g skinless chicken breasts
2 tablespoons vegetable oil
salt and freshly ground black pepper
100 ml sweet chilli sauce
2 large ripe tomatoes
¼ telegraph cucumber or 1 Lebanese
    cucumber
1 avocado, peeled
1 small red onion, very finely sliced

125 g brie cheese, cut into bite-sized
    wedges
80 g or about 4 large handfuls mesclun
    salad
4 tablespoons Roast Garlic Aïoli
    (see page 237)
1 x 140 g packet crispy noodles
    (optional)

Method
Cut the chicken breasts into about 2 cm pieces, toss with the vegetable oil and
season with salt and freshly ground black pepper.

Heat a large frying pan over a moderate heat and cook the chicken pieces in
batches so as not to overcrowd the pan. Cook for 5 minutes, turning once. Return
all chicken pieces to the frying pan and pour over the sweet chilli sauce. Toss well to
coat chicken and then set aside to cool a little.

Cut the tomatoes, cucumber and avocado into about 2 cm chunks.

Place the mesclun onto a large serving platter or 4 serving plates.

Pile the chicken with sauce, tomato, cucumber, avocado, red onion and brie
wedges on top. Serve with the Roast Garlic Aïoli and crispy noodles, if using.

METHOD	SERVES	MEAT	MARINATE	TIME
DEEP FRY	4	**CALAMARI**	**20 MINUTES**	**30 MINUTES**

SPICED CALAMARI

The regulars at the Shepherd's Arms Speight's Ale House in Wellington love this combo – just don't tell them calamari and squid are the same thing or they might try and use it as bait.

Salad
4 tomatoes, cut into chunks
2 Lebanese cucumbers, cut into chunks
1 small red onion, peeled and very
    finely sliced
1–2 tablespoons extra-virgin olive oil
few drops red wine vinegar
12 kalamata olives

salt and freshly ground black pepper
1 thick slice feta cheese, cubed

Calamari
4 calamari tubes (about 150 g each)
½ cup flour
½ tablespoon Cajun seasoning
oil for deep frying

Method
Put tomatoes into a large bowl and add cucumber and red onion. Pour the olive oil over and leave to marinate for about 20 minutes. Meanwhile, prepare the calamari. Take a calamari tube, place a large cook's knife inside the tube and cut tube into a flat sheet. Score the calamari with crisscross cuts and slice into large triangles.

Heat oil in a deep fryer to 190°C.

Mix together the flour and Cajun seasoning. Coat calamari strips with spiced flour mix and cook in batches in the deep fryer. Place some of the strips in the deep fryer basket, then lower the basket into the hot oil and fry until they curl and are golden. Drain on kitchen paper.

Add vinegar and olives to the salad, and a little seasoning, and toss lightly. Scatter the feta cheese on top and serve immediately with hot calamari.

METHOD	SERVES	MEAT	MARINATE	TIME
GRILL/FRY	4	**BEEF**	**1 HOUR**	**30 MINUTES**

ANGUS BEEF SALAD

When it comes to serving the spicy beef with this salad, remember the Southern Man should be generous to a fault.

Thai marinade
1 teaspoon chilli paste or 1 red chilli, seeds removed and finely chopped
1 teaspoon grated fresh ginger
1 clove garlic, crushed
⅓ cup fish sauce
juice of 2 limes
1½ tablespoons brown sugar
2 tablespoons chopped coriander
600–750 g eye fillet or sirloin beef

Method
Combine marinade ingredients in a small bowl.

Cut beef into thin strips and place in a shallow ceramic or glass dish. Pour over the marinade, tossing well. Leave to marinate for one hour.

Thai dressing
4 cloves garlic, crushed
4 teaspoons sugar
8 teaspoons soy sauce
8 teaspoons lemon juice
8 teaspoons fish sauce
4 spring onions, finely sliced
1–2 red chillies, seeds removed and finely chopped
5 teaspoons chopped mint
5 teaspoons chopped parsley
5 teaspoons chopped coriander

Method
Combine all dressing ingredients in a screw-top jar and shake well, or in a bowl and whisk.

Place in a small bowl for serving.

Makes ½ cup.

Continued over . . .

ANGUS BEEF SALAD CONTINUED

Vegetable salad
1 carrot, cut into thin matchsticks
½ red onion, peeled and finely sliced
2 spring onions, finely sliced
½ red capsicum, seeds removed,
    finely sliced

¼ telegraph cucumber, seeds
    removed, sliced
125 g mung bean sprouts, picked over
80 g or about 4 handfuls mesclun salad
4 tablespoons cashew nuts, toasted
100 g crispy noodles

Method
In a large bowl combine the salad vegetables and the cashew nuts.

Heat a large frying pan or grill plate over a high heat. In batches so as not to overcrowd the pan, cook the beef strips quickly on both sides.

To serve: place the salad on a large serving platter of 4 serving plates, scatter over the beef strips and top with the crispy noodles.

Pass the dressing.

Bonspiel, Idaburn, 2010

LIGHT MEAL BEER MATCHING

Seafood
Chowder –
Speight's Gold
Medal Ale

Hearty
Pumpkin Soup
– Speight's
Pilsener

Kumara and
Beetroot Soup
– Speight's
Gold Medal Ale

Ploughman's
Platter –
Speight's
Distinction

Golden
Fritters –
Speight's Gold
Medal Ale

West Coast
Whitebait
Patties –
Speight's Gold
Medal Ale

Chicken Salad
– Speight's
Pilsener

Spiced
Calamari
– Speight's
Summit

Angus Beef
Salad –
Speight's Gold
Medal Ale

Cheese Rolls
– Speight's
Pilsener

The Old
Master's
Cheese Scones
– Speight's
Pilsener

Bealey's
Speight's Pâté –
Speight's
Old Dark

Shuck 'Em
– Speight's
Porter

Southern
Salad –
Speight's
Traverse

Canterbury
Lamb Salad
– Speight's
Traverse

SPEIGHT'S GOLD MEDAL ALE

The true pride of the South, Speight's Gold Medal Ale has been brewed at Speight's Brewery in Dunedin since James Speight, Charles Greenslade and William Dawson set up the brewery in 1876.

Beer style: Draught Amber Ale

First brewed: 1876

Flavour characteristics: Speight's Gold Medal Ale is a classic example of the New Zealand draught beer style, although it is probably less sweet than some if its counterparts. Brewed using three types of hops sourced from Nelson and New Zealand malted barley, Speight's Gold Medal Ale has a distinctive, smooth taste and a malty, biscuity character.

Food match: A great accompaniment to any meat dish and is superb with gamey southern dishes such as venison, duck and rabbit. Perfect with fish and chips.

SPEIGHT'S OLD DARK

Speight's Old Dark has a dark malty character that is similar to old English and Scottish ales. Its sweetish rich flavour has seen it used to make everything from meat pies to chocolates to ice-cream.

Beer style: English Porter

First brewed: 1992

Flavour characteristics: This dark malt ale is brewed with masses of roasted malt. The full-roasted malt flavour has a hint of chocolate and is balanced with extra hops and just enough sweetness.

Food match: The luscious malty and chocolate flavours make it perfect for serving with hot, rich desserts like steamed puddings. Great matched with sweet chocolate desserts. On the savoury side, it goes well with cheese boards, oysters or meat dishes.

SPEIGHT'S SUMMIT LAGER

The summit is where you see nature at its best, where you see things with clarity. It is the view from the top that inspired Speight's Summit Lager. Summit is a refreshing golden lager, brewed with only natural ingredients – after all, you shouldn't mess with nature.

Beer style: Lager

First brewed: June 2008

Flavour characteristics: Brewed with only natural ingredients, Speight's Summit Lager is a smooth lager free of artificial additives and preservatives. With the addition of the Pacific Hallertau hop variety added late in the brew, Speight's Summit Lager delivers a smooth, crisp and refreshing taste with less of the maltiness associated with Speight's Gold Medal Ale.

Food match: Great with lightly battered fish, seafood or spicy dishes.

SPEIGHT'S TRAVERSE LAGER

At Speight's we believe you should only ever carry what you need. So when we started thinking about brewing a low-carb beer, we wanted to make sure it contained only the essentials. That beer is Speight's Traverse.

Beer style: Lager

First brewed: November 2009

Flavour characteristics: A golden lager with a refreshing full flavour and less than half the carbs of regular beers, while containing no artificial additives or preservatives. The slow brewing technique our brewers have perfected keeps the carbs down, while maintaining the full taste we expect from a Speight's beer – the best of both worlds.

Food match: The refreshing full flavour of Speight's Traverse complements light, delicate dishes such as fish, salads and chicken.

SOUTHERN MAN SONG

written by Murray Grindley
often performed by the Southern Man, Denis Henderson

Some of the boys

Got it into their heads

'Bout movin' up north

To follow the bread

That ain't for me

That kind of thing just don't rate

This is one Southern Boy

Who ain't crossin' the Strait

Now I might not be rich

But I like things down here

We got the best looking girls

And the best damn beer

So you can keep your Queen City

With your cocktails and cool

Give me a beer in a seven

With the boys shooting pool

CHORUS

I'm a Southern Man

Well I'm Southern bred

I got the South in my blood

And I'll be here till I'm damn well dead

'Cos here we just know

What makes a Southern boy tick

And it ain't margaritas

With some fruit on a stick

Well it might not be fancy

But when you come from down here

You know you got the best girl

And you got the best beer

HOW TO BE A SOUTHERN MAN

Here it is mate. All you'll ever need to know about Drinking, Dressing, Talking, Driving and thinking Southern Man style.

A SOUTHERN MAN ALWAYS:

- Uses his left hand to drink with, leaving his right hand free to prod the chest of anyone who disagrees with his rugby theories; of which he has an abundance.
- Drives a ute (or a similar no-nonsense wagon) – it has the space for a few kegs of Speight's when the boys come over to watch footy. They're also perfect for hunting and fishing trips or the odd excursion north to support the local team.
- Wears his Speight's jersey with pride whenever he can, especially at his local rugby club or pub.

A SOUTHERN MAN NEVER:

- Eats quiche or beansprouts, uses cellphones or drinks beer out of a stemmed glass.
- He wouldn't be seen dead in a Karaoke Bar and never wears boat shoes (except on a boat).
- Holds hands with his woman in public nor ride scooters or mopeds.

FOOD – THE SOUTHERN MAN PREFERS:

- A barbeque at the back of the flat with the boys telling a few lies over a cold Speight's.
- Good curries; the hotter the better, as well as raw Bluff oysters, whitebait and good meat pies.
- Wild pork on the spit, venison sausages and white bread, giblet soup and roasts are all his favourites.
- Not to patronise restaurants that don't serve jugs.
- Muttonbird stew.

ANIMALS – THE SOUTHERN MAN WON'T TOLERATE:

- Any animal you can't ride, throw a rope on or muster sheep with.

THE SOUTHERN MAN RESPECTS:

- Women who drink Speight's out of a jug.
- Laurie Mains.

HOLIDAYS — WHILE ON HOLIDAY THE SOUTHERN MAN...

- Only goes where he can get Speight's.
- Is disturbed about the trend where Speight's is becoming available in more Northern provinces as he has no excuse when pressured by his wife to travel out of the South.
- Doesn't allow his wife to drive unless he's had a few.
- Looks forward to getting back to his favourite bar.

SPORT – THE SOUTHERN MAN...

- Plays any contact sport where there is risk to life or limb.
- Watches and talks rugby, even during the cricket season.
- Referees rugby (from the terraces at Carisbrook).
- Doesn't switch on the cricket until Ken Rutherford is batting.
- Only travels to Auckland for test matches and then only if he can drink Speight's.
- Enjoys John Hart and Richard Loe jokes and is convinced that it's only a coincidence that so many of the present All-Black team are current or former Otago players.
- Always questions any Aucklanders selected in a national team and remembers Grizz Wylie's and Laurie Mains' birthdays.
- Thinks basketball is the name for netball when men play it.

CLOTHES – THE SOUTHERN MAN...

- Prefers practical clothing eg Swanndris, Levi jeans, rugby jerseys and shirts with padded elbows for leaning on his favourite bar.
- Unlike Aucklanders, he doesn't own more than two ties (preferably rugby club ties) and he wouldn't be seen dead in a skivvy or cardigan.
- Doesn't wear choker chains, rings or ear studs.

THE LINGO

- "Scarffie" = University student
- "One for the road" = Two for the road
- "McGann" = Beer pot
- "Sip" = 5 jugs
- "Big sip" = In excess of 8 jugs
- "Spiggits/Real beer" = Speight's Gold Medal Ale
- "A wee bit nippy" = 6 degree frost

IN GENERAL – SOUTHERN MEN:

- Never sit down in public bars.
- Never ask to see the wine list.
- Will never leave beer in his glass
- Are respected wherever they go, for their taste in clothes, their taste in sport, and of course their taste in beer

SPEIGHT'S
Pride of the South

Southern Man poster from the early 1990s

THE DEVOTED HIGHLANDER

The motto for the 93rd Argyll and Sutherland Highlanders regiment of the British army is Ne Obliviscaris – Do Not Forget. One of their number, a chap called Danny Wilton, took that motto very literally after visiting Dunedin for the New Zealand and South Seas Exhibition in 1925.

The exhibition was a big deal for the city as it brought people from all over the world to check out what the city – and the country – had to offer. More than three million people visited the exhibition while it was on, which was pretty amazing given that New Zealand's population was well under half that number at the time.

Speight's has always been renowned for providing fantastic hospitality and 1925 was no different. Charles Speight was one of the main organisers of the exhibition and he wanted to make sure everyone visiting the exhibition had a great time. Speight's produced a special bottling ale with a commemorative label as well as having a stand at the exhibition.

With all those people visiting Logan Park, the organisers made sure that there was plenty of entertainment to keep them amused. The Argyll and Sutherland Highlanders military band came out from Britain and performed every day for the 24 weeks that the exhibition ran. Now the Highlanders were a pretty staunch bunch of blokes and their trip to Dunedin wouldn't have been the first time they'd encountered Kiwis. During the First World War they fought alongside each other at Gallipoli, and on the Western Front in France and Belgium.

During the months of the exhibition, Charles Speight got to know some of the fellas in the band quite well. After they left Dunedin, they were supposed to go to the United States to continue their tour, but the trip got cancelled. They had to head home as soon as possible, which meant that they had to take whatever transport they could. When Charles Speight heard that his Highlander mates were due to leave Wellington in the hold of a cargo ship, he was furious. Being a hands-on kind of bloke, he inspected the ship and made sure that conditions were improved as much as they could be before the Highlanders headed home.

One of the Highlanders, Danny Wilton (who was actually a Londoner), really took the regimental motto to heart – he didn't forget Dunedin or Speight's. As soon as he was discharged he sailed straight back to Dunedin and got himself a job as malt-house worker at Speight's. One of the perks of the job was that Danny could indulge in his favourite drop at smoko (how times have changed!) and he was famous for having ten glasses of beer lined up ready for him when he knocked off for his break. He'd drink them down and go back to work quite happily.

Danny's life in the military wasn't quite over – he was called up and served in the Second World War before going back to his job at the brewery. You might think that the effects of fighting in two world wars, juggling working at the brewery with playing in the local movie theatre orchestra and supping considerable amounts of beer each day might leave Danny with a bit of a weak constitution . . . not likely! Danny Wilton was famous for working for Speight's for more than forty years without a single day off sick. Now that's dedication to the job! He was also known for turning up for the nightshift still in his penguin suit after playing in the cinema orchestra!

CRYSTAL MALT
B/N 23.1129
CRYER MALT
USE NO HOO
CRYSTAL MA
B/N 23.1129
CRYER MALT
TRALIA
CRYSTAL MALT
B/N 23.1129
CRYER MALT
USE NO HOOKS
KEEP DRY & COOL
25 kg NET
RYSTAL MALT
B/N 23.1129
CRYER MALT
USE NO HOOKS
KEEP DRY & COO
25 kg NET

ANYWHERE NORTH OF
HERE IS NOWHERE.

Lindis Pass, Central Otago

Wedderburn Hotel, Maniototo

PIES

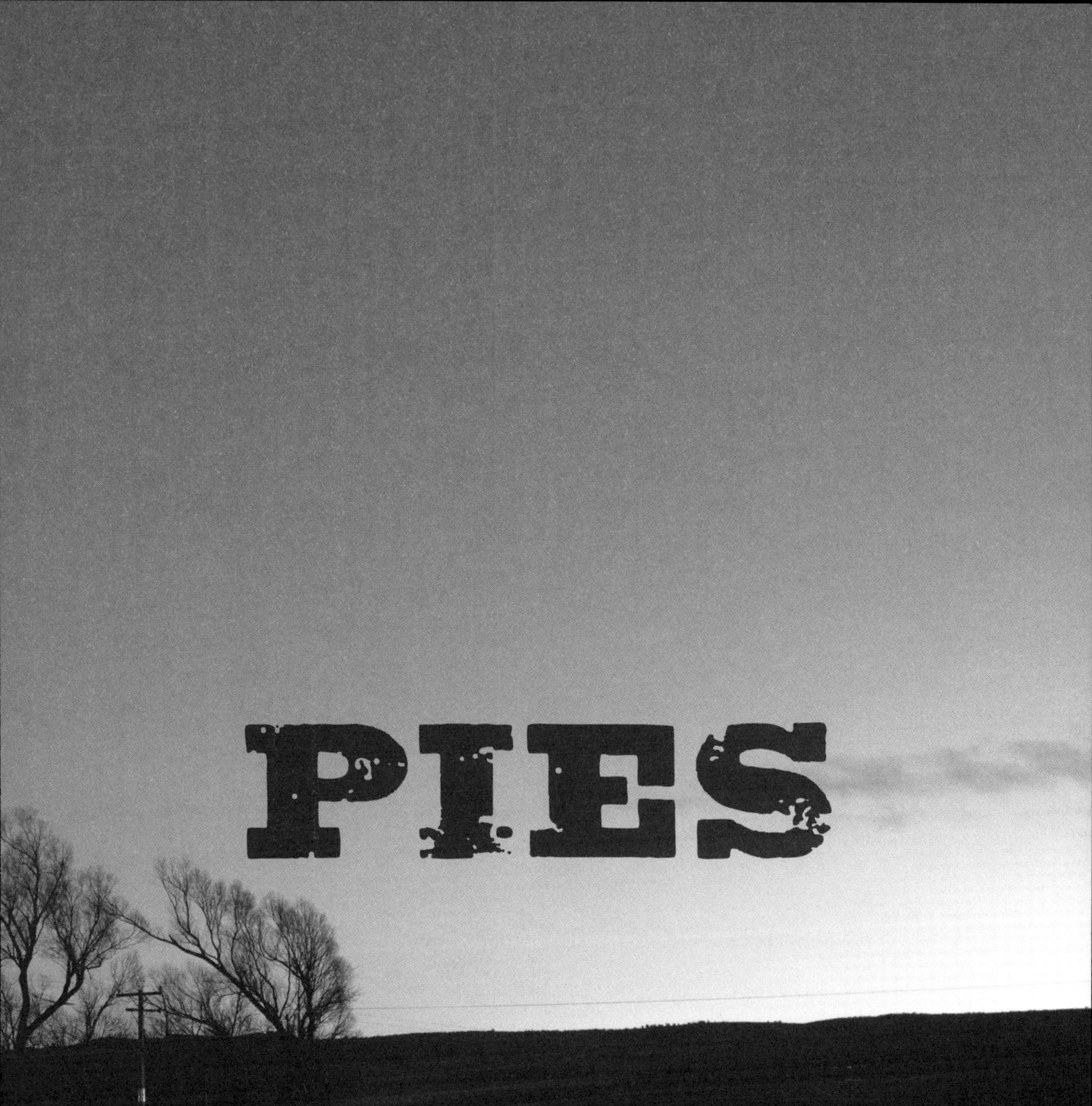

METHOD	SERVES	MEAT	TIME
FRY/BAKE	4	**BEEF**	**4-4½ HOURS**

DISTINCTION PIE

Southern Men tend not to mince their words, nor a fine cut of rump. Get your teeth into this hearty pie.

1 tablespoon vegetable oil
4 small onions, finely sliced
4 cloves garlic, crushed
1 kg beef rump, cut into 2 cm chunks
50 g butter, plus 15 g extra
3 tablespoons flour
1 x 330 ml bottle Speight's
    Distinction beer

125 ml beef stock
salt and freshly ground black pepper
bouquet garni (1 bay leaf, 3 sprigs
    thyme and a few parsley stalks tied
    together with natural string)
700 g button mushrooms
3 sheets pre-rolled puff pastry
2 egg yolks, lightly beaten, for egg glaze

Method

Preheat the oven to 150–160°C.

In a large frying pan, heat the oil and add the onions and garlic. Cook gently until soft, about 5 minutes. Transfer to an ovenproof casserole dish.

Brown the beef pieces on both sides in batches, so as not to overcrowd the pan. Put with the onions and garlic.

Add 50 g of butter to the frying pan then stir in the flour to make a roux. Cook for 30 seconds. Pour in the beer and beef stock. Bring to the boil, season with salt and freshly ground black pepper and pour into the casserole dish. Drop in the bouquet garni, cover with the lid and place in the preheated oven for 2½–3 hours until the beef is tender. Leave to cool.

Meanwhile, cook the mushrooms in 15 g butter for 1–2 minutes. Add to the beef casserole and increase oven temperature to 180°C.

Line the base and sides of a 20 cm square tin with 2 sheets of pre-rolled pastry. (Roll the 2 sheets together to fit the tin.)

Put in the filling, brush edges with a little of the egg glaze and cover with the remaining sheet of pastry. Crimp edges and brush with egg glaze. Make 2–3 slits in the top with a sharp knife to allow steam to escape.

Bake for 35–40 minutes or until the pastry is a good golden colour.

METHOD	SERVES	MEAT	TIME
FRY/BAKE	4	**CHICKEN**	**60 MINUTES**

THREE-STAR PIE

There's nothing quite like a good chick'n'mush pie to accompany a cold Speight's. Tamara Smith from Speight's Ale House Palmerston North makes the ultimate chick'n'mush.

½ cup flour
salt and freshly ground black pepper
500 g skinless chicken breasts, cut into
    2 cm chunks
2 tablespoons olive oil
25 g butter
1 onion, finely chopped or 2 small leeks,
    white part only, sliced
2 cloves garlic, crushed
125 g mushrooms, sliced

⅓ cup white wine
1 cup chicken stock
½ cup cream
1 teaspoon wholegrain mustard
1 tablespoon chopped fresh herbs
    (tarragon is good)
1 tablespoon chopped parsley
4 sheets pre-rolled puff pastry
2 eggs, lightly beaten, for glaze

Method

Put flour, salt and black pepper in a bowl and mix. Add chicken and toss well.

Heat oil and butter in a large frying pan over a moderate to high heat. Shake excess flour off chicken and cook in batches until golden and sealed (not cooked all the way through). Transfer chicken to a plate and set aside.

Place the onion or leeks and garlic in the frying pan and cook gently until soft, about 5 minutes. Add the mushrooms and cook for 1 minute. Add wine and boil for 1 minute then add the stock and cream and simmer for a further 5 minutes.

Remove from the heat, add chicken, mustard and herbs and set aside to cool.

Preheat the oven to 180°C. Cut pastry to line bases and tops of 4 x 10–11 cm pie tins.

Spoon the filling into pastry cases. Brush edges of pastry with egg glaze. Place tops on pies and seal with a fork or crimp with your thumb. Brush tops with egg glaze. Make 2–3 slits with a sharp knife in the top of each pie to allow steam to escape.

Place pies in the preheated oven and cook for 35 minutes or until golden.

METHOD	SERVES	MEAT	TIME
FRY/BAKE	4	**BACON**	**50 MINUTES**

MRS O'DONNELL'S BACON AND EGG PIE

According to Mrs O'Donnell this pie is a favourite with her boys. She also reckons that there's no place for peas in a bacon and egg pie. She's an honest woman, Mrs O.

250 g streaky bacon, chopped
2 sheets pre-rolled flaky puff pastry
2 tablespoons chopped parsley (optional)
1 teaspoon chopped chives (optional)

6 eggs
freshly ground black pepper
1 egg, lightly beaten with a pinch of
    salt, for glaze

Method
Preheat the oven to 190°C.

Lightly fry the bacon and leave to cool.

Roll the first sheet of pastry to fit an enamel pie plate, working the pastry up the side of the dish. Roll the other sheet of pastry to make a lid and put aside.

Scatter two-thirds of the bacon over the base of the pie, then scatter half of the chopped parsley and chives over the base, if using. Break eggs over the top of the bacon. Season with freshly ground black pepper and add remaining herbs, if using. Add remaining bacon, taking care to avoid breaking the egg yolks. Cover with the other pastry sheet. Crimp together the edges with your thumb. Brush with egg glaze and make 2–3 slits in the pastry to allow steam to escape.

Place in the preheated oven and cook for 30–35 minutes.

Serve with tomato sauce.

SPEIGHT'S ALE HOUSE DUNEDIN

The first hotel built on the site of the Speight's Ale House in Dunedin was the Shamrock. It was built in 1862 by a couple of American brothers, the Murphys. Now the Murphys ran a pretty sharp joint with oak walls, glass chandeliers and gold decorations – not your usual Southern Man kind of a place. When James Speight, William Dawson and Charles Greenslade built their brewery next door, there was a bit of a win-win for both businesses. Speight's used the Shamrock to hold meetings and other functions. But not for long.

In 1882, the Shamrock came into the ownership of the Presbyterian Church who weren't all that keen to be running a pub, so they leased the place to Speight's. This happy arrangement lasted for 20 years until the church were no longer able to face the fact that they were benefiting from the sale of the 'demon drink'. The lease was cancelled and the hotel became an auction rooms, and the licence was transferred to the Clarendon Hotel just around the corner.

Eventually, Speight's bought the Shamrock and demolished the old hotel. Robert Forrest designed a new building for the site, which was built in 1912–13. This new Shamrock Building became part of the rapidly expanding brewery. The space the Ale House now occupies was once the brewery's engineers' workshop.

The Shamrock Building remained just another part of the brewery until 1999. That was when someone at Speight's had a really good idea. 'Let's build a pub at the brewery!' And so they did.

Once they'd decided to build the pub, they needed to find someone to lease the place from them and run it. They didn't have to look very far. Working for the company at the time was a bloke by the name of Mark Scully. A Southlander by birth, Mark had gone from studying at Otago University to working for Speight's. He was the perfect candidate to run this new pub, and he's been behind the bar at the Ale House ever since.

It opened for business on 28 October 1999 and was declared officially open on 15 November by Prime Minister Jenny Shipley.

When the bar first opened, there was a choice of Speight's Gold Medal Ale (or Speight's as it's known down south), Old Dark or Distinction. It was a bit of a risk not having a lager but it didn't seem to make any difference, with 93 per cent of punters opting for a Speight's straight from the tap. That's probably because it doesn't get fresher than at the Ale House. The beers come from right next door.

Fresh is best doesn't just apply to the beer at the Ale House either. The food there is local and seasonal. The restaurant opened with about 40 seats but it wasn't long before word got out about how good the food is and there's a whole lot more chairs in there now.

Mark and his wife Kirstin ran the place so successfully that before long the company started to look at opening Ale Houses around the rest of the country. As the new Ale Houses opened, Mark provided guidance to the new owners, garnering him the well-earned nickname 'the Godfather'.

METHOD	SERVES	MEAT	TIME
BAKE	4	**FISH**	**50 MINUTES**

FOVEAUX FISH PIE

When Speight's Ale House Invercargill held a recipe competition in 2009, Southern Man Wade Millar was a clear winner with his Foveaux Fish Pie. Good on ya, Wade.

4 eggs
50 g butter, plus extra for buttering dish
1 small onion, finely chopped
3 tablespoons flour
2 cups milk, plus extra if needed
salt and freshly ground black pepper
1 tablespoon chopped parsley

300 g firm white fish fillets, cut into
   2 cm pieces
300 g smoked fish fillets, flaked into
   about 2 cm pieces
6 basil leaves, torn
1 cup grated cheddar cheese
1 cup breadcrumbs

Method

Preheat the oven to 190°C. Lightly butter a 20 cm ovenproof baking dish.

Bring a saucepan of water to boil then boil the eggs for 7 minutes. Drain, run eggs under cold water until cold then peel.

Melt butter in a saucepan, add the onion and cook gently until soft, about 5 minutes. Add flour and stir. Allow the mixture to bubble gently, stirring continuously until lightly golden.

Add the milk to the mixture, a ½ cup at a time. Whisk continuously, until all the milk has been added and the sauce is thick enough to coat the back of a wooden spoon. Season with salt and black pepper and stir the parsley through.

Place the fish into the baking dish. Slice or quarter the eggs and place on top.

Pour sauce over the top and sprinkle torn basil leaves on top. Mix the cheese and breadcrumbs together and sprinkle on top.

Place in the preheated oven and cook for 20 minutes until the topping is golden.`

Serve with a green salad or steamed vegetables.

METHOD	SERVES	MEAT	TIME
BAKE	4	**LAMB**	**1½ HOURS**

SHEPHERD'S PIE

The English used to make Shepherd's Pie with meat left over from a roast. With a Southern Man in the house there's never any leftovers so us Kiwis make it with prime fresh lamb mince.

Base
1 tablespoon vegetable oil
1 onion, peeled and chopped
1 carrot, peeled and chopped
2 sticks celery, lightly peeled to remove stringy bits and chopped
6 brown mushrooms, sliced
500 g lamb mince
1 x 400 g can chopped tomatoes in juice
½–1 cup beef stock

4–5 drops Worcestershire sauce
1 teaspoon tomato paste
salt and freshly ground black pepper

Potato topping
3 large floury potatoes, such as Agria or Ilam Hardy, peeled and cut into even-sized pieces
1 teaspoon salt
⅓ cup hot milk
25 g butter

Method

Start with the base. Put the oil, chopped onion, carrot, celery and mushrooms in a large saucepan. Cook over a low heat for about 5 minutes until the onion is soft.

Add the lamb mince, turn up the heat and cook for 5 minutes, stirring until the mince begins to brown.

Add the chopped tomatoes, beef stock, Worcestershire sauce, tomato paste and season with salt and freshly ground black pepper. Simmer, covered, for 20 minutes then uncover and cook for a further 5–10 minutes until most of the liquid is absorbed.

While the mince is simmering, put potatoes in a large saucepan. Cover with water, add salt and boil until tender, about 20 minutes.

Preheat the oven to 190°C. Lightly grease a 23 cm ovenproof baking dish.

Drain the cooked potatoes and dry off over the heat, shaking the saucepan, until the potatoes appear dry. Mash the potatoes then, using a wooden spoon, beat in the hot milk a little at a time, then the butter. Beat thoroughly.

Put the cooked lamb mince into the prepared dish. Pile the mashed potato on top, then fork up the potato to give a rough surface. Place in the preheated oven and cook for 25 minutes until the potato is golden.

METHOD	SERVES	MEAT	TIME
BAKE	10–20	**VENISON**	**2½ HOURS**

MRS MCCONNELL'S VENISON PIES

There are some as think that without Mrs McConnell's Venison Pie, no-one would ever bother buying tickets to the annual Deerstalkers' Ball. Admittedly they're McConnells too, but they've got a strong case.

250 g bacon, chopped into 2 cm chunks
1 medium onion, finely diced
2 carrots, peeled and sliced
2 sticks celery, lightly peeled to remove stringy bits, sliced
4 cloves garlic, crushed
4 tablespoons chopped herbs, such as thyme, rosemary, sage and parsley
½ cup flour
salt and freshly ground black pepper

1 kg venison, cut into 2 cm chunks
1 tablespoon vegetable oil
½ cup port
1–1½ cups beef stock
1 x 330 ml bottle Speight's Distinction beer
100 g kumara, peeled and cut into about 1 cm chunks
10 sheets pre-rolled flaky puff pastry
2 egg whites, lightly beaten
2 egg yolks, lightly beaten

Method

In a large heavy-based saucepan over a moderate heat fry the bacon until golden, about 5 minutes.

Add the onion, carrot, celery, garlic and herbs. Cook gently for about 10 minutes.

Place flour seasoned with salt and freshly ground black pepper into a bowl. Add venison and toss well.

Heat the oil in a large frying pan, shake excess flour off the venison and brown on both sides. Add to the vegetables.

Pour port into the frying pan and scrape up any meaty bits and add this to the vegetables and venison. Add stock and beer, whisk in any remaining seasoned flour and bring to the boil.

Turn heat to low and simmer gently for 1½ hours, stirring occasionally. Remove the lid for the last 30 minutes to allow the sauce to reduce.

Add the kumara and cook for a further 10 minutes. Taste for seasoning then set aside to cool.

Continued over . . .

MRS MCCONNELL'S VENISON PIES CONTINUED

Preheat the oven to 180°C.

Put sheets of pastry on a lightly floured surface in a production line. Using a plate or bowl about 11–12 cm wide, cut out 40 circles.

Place a large spoonful of meat mixture in the centre of 20 circles, leaving a 2 cm edge.

Brush the edges with egg white and place the remaining rounds on top. Pinch 5 evenly placed crimps on the top pastry rounds then fold up the base and pinch pastry together.

Place pies on shallow baking trays lined with baking paper and chill for 10–15 minutes. Brush the tops with egg yolk glaze. Make 2–3 slits in the top of each pie with a sharp knife to allow steam to escape.

Place in preheated oven and cook for 25 minutes until a good golden colour.

Makes 20 pies.

SOUTHERN MAN IDENTIFICATION CHART.

In these trying times of rugby losses to the Australians and naked chefs, it's time we mentioned and reminded ourselves of the types of men (and their dogs) that make this country great.

Hat - Practical, rugged and never, ever worn backwards.

Teeth - Firmly gritted whenever accidentally exposed to 'Boy Band' or "Pop Princess" while searching for sport.

Jaw - Dropped when he heard ballroom dancing was made an Olympic sport.

Heart - Placed firmly in the South, even when reluctantly traveling north of Waitaki.

Right Hand - Holds rugby balls, rifles, shearing equipment, BBQ tongs, tools and a Footy mag in a firm manly grip.

Dog - Responds to calls of "Dog" and "Ya Bloody Mongrel". Has never been in a perfumed bath (unless you count the sheep dip in the trough).

Brow - Slightly furrowed from contemplating why Aucklanders need four wheel drives to get up Queen Street

Mouth - Where the Speight's goes.

Chest - Swells with pride whenever passing the Brook or Speight's Brewery

Left Hand - The only hand from which Speight's is traditionally drunk.

Body - Never adorned in lycra, skivvies, cardigans or fabric that doesn't scratch.

Knees - Often found bent in prayer during the last few minutes of a close test.

Feet - Occasionally connect with the rear end of dogs, sheep, cattle and designer beer drinkers.

Pride of the South

REMEMBER THE CORRECT WAY TO GREET A SOUTHERN MAN IS "GOOD ON YA MATE, HAVE A SPEIGHT'S ON ME".

Southern Man poster from the 1990s

METHOD	SERVES	MEAT	TIME
SIMMER/ BAKE	**6**	**RABBIT**	**2–2½ HOURS**

RABBIT PIE

The Southern Man knows that the only good rabbit is a dead one. And the rabbit in this pie is a bloody good one!

Pie
1 rabbit
2 litres chicken stock
1 stick celery, chopped
1 carrot, chopped
1 onion, sliced
1 bay leaf
2 sprigs thyme
3–4 parsley stalks
a few black peppercorns
125 g rindless streaky bacon, chopped
200 g button mushrooms, sliced

½ cup chopped parsley
12 sheets filo pastry (1 x 375 g packet)
melted butter for brushing
sesame seeds for sprinkling

Sauce
75 g butter
75 g flour
600 ml stock from cooking rabbit
100 ml cream
juice of 1 lemon
salt and freshly ground black pepper

Method
If using store-bought rabbit, remove the kidneys that will be tucked inside. Place rabbit in a large saucepan with the stock, celery, carrot, onion, herbs and peppercorns and simmer for 1–1½ hours, or until the back legs are tender. Allow rabbit to cool in the stock.

Remove rabbit and strain stock. Set aside. Remove meat from the bones and cut into small pieces.

In a frying pan, lightly cook the bacon, then the mushrooms. Place in a bowl.

Lightly brown the kidneys on both sides and remove from pan. Chop the kidneys and mix with rabbit meat, bacon, mushrooms and chopped parsley. Cover and set aside.

To make the sauce, cook butter and flour over a gentle heat until a light golden colour. Gradually add the reserved stock and cook about 10 minutes, stirring continuously until thick. Add cream and lemon juice. Season with salt and freshly ground black pepper.

Add enough sauce to the meat to make a creamy but not sloppy filling.

Preheat the oven to 180°C.

Line a 28 cm x 18 cm sponge roll tin with 6 sheets filo pastry, brushing with butter between each sheet.

Spoon filling in and top with another 6 sheets filo pastry, brushed with butter. Butter the top and sprinkle with sesame seeds. Put into the oven and cook 20–30 minutes until the filo pastry is a good golden colour.

Serve hot with mashed potato flavoured with chopped parsley or some basil pesto and baby leeks or carrots.

PIES BEER MATCHING

Distinction
Pie – Speight's
Distinction

Three
Star Pie –
Speight's
Pilsener

Mrs O'Donnell's
Bacon and Egg
Pie – Speight's
Gold Medal
Ale

Foveaux
Fish Pie –
Speight's
Pilsener

Classic
Shepherd's
Pie – Speight's
Gold Medal
Ale

Mrs McConnell's
Venison Pies
– Speight's
Distinction

Rabbit Pie –
Speight's Gold
Medal Ale

Bonspiel, Idaburn, 2010

SOUTHERN FRUGALITY

The Scots, who made up the bulk of the first European settlers in Otago, were renowned for their frugality. They sure knew how to make their pennies stretch as far as they could.

Only one of the founders of Speight's was a Scotsman – William Dawson would certainly be proud that Speight's has survived for more than 130 years and he'd be especially proud of the fact that nothing in the brewery goes to waste. In fact, most of what the brewery produces is reused or recycled in some way.

Ever since the brewery first opened, Speight's beer has been sent out into the world in recyclable packaging. In the early days all the beer was sold in wooden casks that were returned to the brewery empty before being washed and refilled. Before long, Speight's was being sold in glass bottles which would be collected up and recycled in traditional Kiwi fund-raising bottle drives. Then, in the 1950s, came the ultimate in minimal packaging – the beer tanker. The truck would be pumped full of beer and then be driven to a pub where its precious cargo would be dispensed into waiting tanks and from there into waiting patrons. Then came the refillable metal keg, which if it wasn't returned to be refilled would sometimes end up recycled as slightly uncomfortable furniture in a student flat. In 1984 Speight's started to be sold in cans and, you guessed it, the cans are recyclable too.

It's not just the beer packaging that gets reused either. Beer only has four main ingredients and what Speight's does with those ingredients is pretty interesting –

and not just in the beer-making sense. At the brewery in Dunedin, all the water used in brewing comes from a bore directly under the brewery. There are no transport costs and it couldn't be purer or come from closer to the source. Speight's has been using the same parent source of yeast for 50 years, which is equivalent to the average length of time a Southern Man will wear a Swanndri before considering replacing it.

There are a couple of products used in the brewing process that are left over once the beer has been brewed. The first of these is yeast. During the fermenting process yeast multiplies hugely and at the end of each brewing there's always quite a bit left over. What happens to this might surprise you. Next time you sit down to breakfast you should feel happy that your favourite breakfast spread contains the excess yeast from your favourite beer. Yep, that leftover yeast gets sold to Sanitarium who use it to make Marmite.

The other product that is left over after the brewing process is the malted grain. Having done its work in the beer, the remains of the grain is sold to local farmers who use it to feed some of the healthiest, happiest cattle in the country.

With all this recycling and reusing, some people might even describe the brewery as a bit green. But Hugh Speight, who ran the brewery for quite a few years, absolutely detested the colour green so let's just say that Speight's tries its best to be aware of the environment.

Gyle room, Speight's Brewery, Dunedin

Patearoa Road, near Waipiata

PASTA

METHOD	SERVES	MEAT	TIME
FRY/BOIL	4	**BACON**	**25 MINUTES**

WILD MUSHROOM AND BACON FETTUCCINE

Here's an emergency recipe, just in case there are no potatoes – in the whole town. True field mushrooms pop up after the first autumn rain. The best place to collect mushies for this recipe is from a grazed paddock where heaps of cow manure has been applied.

6 rashers bacon (or wild hog if on hand),
   cut into strips
50 g butter
1 medium onion, very finely sliced
2–3 cloves garlic, finely chopped
400 g field mushrooms, wiped clean and
   cut if large

1 cup cream
400 g fresh fettuccine
salt and freshly ground pepper
Parmesan cheese for serving, if using

Method
Heat a large frying pan and cook bacon strips until crisp. Set aside on a plate.

Put the butter and onion into the frying pan and cook 5–10 minutes until the onion is soft. Add the garlic and the mushrooms and cook for 4–6 minutes, stirring occasionally.

Add the cream and simmer for 5 minutes, until the cream thickens to a sauce consistency.

Meanwhile, cook the pasta in a large saucepan of boiling salted water for 3 minutes until al dente or as per instructions on the packet. Drain well.

Drop the cooked fettuccine into the creamy sauce and season with salt and freshly ground black pepper.

Toss well and place into warmed pasta bowls. Top with the bacon strips and serve with Parmesan cheese, if desired.

SOUTHERN MEN
DON'T EAT PASTA

Wedderburn, Central Otago

MAINS

METHOD	SERVES	MEAT	MARINATE	TIME
GRILL/ BARBECUE	4	**PORK OR BEEF**	**AT LEAST 1 HOUR**	**25 MINUTES**

ARRAN'S SORE RIBS

After 111 games for Otago and 15 All Black tests, Arran Pene knows a few things about sore ribs. Thankfully, now, as the boss at the Speight's Ale House in Hamilton, he just gets to serve them up. He recommends allowing about six spare ribs per person, but you could double that for hungry musterers.

1 kg spare ribs, pork or beef
1 x 330 ml bottle Speight's Old Dark
  beer
¼ cup orange juice

½ cup smoky barbecue sauce
⅓ cup malt vinegar
6–8 cloves garlic, crushed
1 tablespoon grated fresh ginger

Method
Cut the spare ribs into lengths, cutting between each rib to separate them.

Mix together the beer, orange juice, barbecue sauce, malt vinegar, garlic and ginger. Pour into a sealable plastic bag, add the spare ribs, seal and toss to coat. Allow to marinate for at least an hour. Overnight in the fridge is better.

Preheat the oven on fan grill to 200°C. Line a shallow baking dish or oven tray with two layers of foil.

Drain off and reserve the marinade. Place the spare ribs on the prepared tray making sure they are in a single layer.

Cook under the preheated grill for 15 minutes, turning occasionally and at the same time brushing with the marinade until the spare ribs are well browned.

Alternatively, barbecue the ribs over a moderate grill plate, brushing with the reserved marinade regularly.

METHOD	SERVES	MEAT	MARINATE	TIME
GRILL/ BARBECUE	4	**BEEF**	**8 HOURS**	**6–8 MINUTES**

RATTRAY STEAK

If a Southern Man ever finds himself in the big smoke, he'll pay a visit to the original Speight's Ale House for a Rattray Steak to build up his strength before he has to risk his life on that bloody one-way system again.

2 x 330 ml bottles Speight's Old Dark
200 ml tomato sauce
3 tablespoons brown sugar
3 tablespoons Worcestershire sauce

1 tablespoon crushed garlic
12 sprigs fresh thyme
4 x 250 g rump steaks

Method
In a bowl combine all ingredients except the meat.

Place the rump steak in a shallow ceramic or glass dish and pour the marinade over and stir to cover the meat. Marinate for at least 8 hours.

Heat a grill plate to high and grill steaks for 3-4 minutes on each side for medium-rare steak.

Serve with fries and salad and some wholegrain mustard on the side.

METHOD	SERVES	MEAT	TIME
SLOW COOK	4	**LAMB**	**9 HOURS**

SHEARERS' SHANKS

After a day in the sheds, shearers are always absolutely starving. A big feed of shanks and a few tonnes of mash might just fill the gap.

1 tablespoon olive oil
2 onions, chopped
2 carrots, peeled and chopped
4 cloves garlic, crushed
4 sprigs fresh thyme
1 bay leaf
A few parsley stalks

4 lamb shanks
100 ml red wine
1 x 400 g can chopped tomatoes in juice
1 tablespoon tomato paste
2 cups boiling water
salt and freshly ground black pepper
butter and flour to thicken sauce

Method

Heat olive oil in a large frying pan, add onion, carrot, and garlic and cook gently for about 5 minutes.

Place in the base of a slow cooker. Sprinkle herbs on top.

Place a frying pan over a moderate heat and brown the lamb shanks on all sides, then place on top of herbs.

Add red wine to the frying pan and allow to bubble up. Add tomatoes and juice and tomato paste. Pour in boiling water and stir well. Season with salt and freshly ground black pepper.

Pour over the lamb shanks. (The liquid should just cover the shanks.) Turn slow cooker to low and cook for 8 hours until the lamb is beginning to fall off the bone.

Remove lamb shanks and strain sauce through a sieve, pushing down on the vegetables as you go. Leave to cool to allow the fat to rise to the surface and set. Remove fat.

Reheat the lamb shanks in the sauce. Thicken sauce by whisking in a paste of equal quantities of softened butter and flour, until the sauce is a syrupy consistency. Taste and season to taste with salt and freshly ground black pepper.

Serve lamb shanks with your favourite mash and steamed vegetables.

METHOD	SERVES	MEAT	TIME
FRY	4	**LAMB**	**20 MINUTES**

GRANDMA'S LAMB'S FRY

Grandma was a good old stick and if there was one thing she knew how to do, it was cook up some tasty lamb's fry.

1 tablespoon olive oil
1 onion, thinly sliced
4 thick rashers streaky bacon
¼ cup flour

salt and freshly ground black pepper
4–8 slices lamb's liver, skinned
3 tablespoons beef stock

Method

Heat a frying pan over a low heat and add the olive oil. Cook the onion for about 10 minutes until soft and lightly golden. Remove from pan and keep warm.

Cook the bacon until crisp, then put with the onion and keep warm.

Place flour on a flat plate, season with salt and black pepper. Dip liver in the seasoned flour and shake off excess.

Add liver slices to the hot pan and cook 2–3 minutes on both sides until browned.

Remove liver to a serving plate, pour stock into the pan, heat, then pour pan juices over the liver and serve at once with the onion and bacon. A bit of toast on the side is mighty nice too.

METHOD	SERVES	MEAT	MARINATE	TIME
GRILL/ BARBECUE	6	**LAMB**	**2 DAYS**	**15 MINUTES**

HIGHLAND LAMB

The Southern Man is economical with his words, but a feed of Highland Lamb will elicit a heartfelt 'beaut' from him – for sure.

1 cup olive oil
1 tablespoon paprika (preferably bittersweet Spanish paprika)
½ tablespoon ground cumin

1 teaspoon New York pepper (see below)
4–5 garlic cloves, crushed
6 lamb backstraps

Method
For best results, the lamb needs to be marinated for 2 days.
In a small bowl, combine the oil, paprika, cumin, New York pepper and garlic.
Place the lamb backstraps in a shallow ceramic or glass dish and pour over the marinade. Leave to marinate for as long as possible, up to 2 days.
Heat a grill plate to high and cook lamb for 4 minutes on each side. Leave to rest on a warm plate, covered loosely with tin foil, for 5 minutes.

Tip: To make New York pepper, combine ¼ cup cracked peppercorns (not ground) with 3 tablespoons lime or lemon pepper seasoning. Store in an airtight container.

METHOD	SERVES	MEAT	TIME
BARBECUE	4	**BEEF**	**20 MINUTES**

SOUTHERN MAN'S MINCEMEAT

For the Southern Man, a drive-through is a half-flooded river, a takeaway is a tin full of scones and a Thermos of soup from his mum, and supersizing is what he does to get in shape for the rugby season.

600 g beef mince
1 small onion, finely chopped
2 eggs
1 teaspoon Dijon mustard
1 teaspoon Worcestershire sauce

2–3 dashes Tabasco sauce, optional
1 tablespoon chopped parsley
1 tablespoon chopped coriander
salt and freshly ground black pepper

Method
In a large bowl combine all the ingredients together, mixing well. The best way to do this is with your hands.

Divide the mixture into 4 and with wet hands shape into round patties.

Cook on a preheated barbecue hotplate or in a large lightly oiled frying pan until well browned on both sides and firm to the touch.

SPEIGHT'S ALE HOUSE INVERCARGILL

Down in Invercargill, they've always done things a bit differently from the rest of the country. At the southern end of the South Island, luncheon sausage is called belgium, vacuuming is called luxing and dents are called dints. Mind you, ask a Southlander and they'll tell you it's the rest of the country who have got it wrong!

Another way that Invercargill manages to set itself apart from the rest of the country is in the fact that you'd expect the southernmost Ale House to be run by a good old Southern Man. Well, you can expect that all you like but don't tell Stephanie Bekhuis.

Stephanie, with her offsider Marina Fonoti, runs the Invercargill Speight's Ale House and has done so very successfully since November 2006. Before taking over the reins as the first female Ale House manager, Stephanie had worked in all sorts of hospitality roles and she knows a thing or two about how to run a great pub – some might even say she's the 'Perfect Woman'.

The building that is home to Invercargill's Speight's Ale House was built in the late 1800s. For most of last century, the building was home to a shoe shop. The good ladies of Invercargill who bought their shoes there would have been hard pressed to imagine the fantastic indoor/ outdoor barbeque that is now at home upstairs. They would, however, have recognised many of the dishes on the Ale House menu including the most delicious of Southern seasonal goodies like Bluff oysters and local duck.

You'll find venison on the menu at the Speight's Ale House Invercargill but it's also possible that you'll find another kind of Stag in the pub. The Southland rugby team, the Stags, are sponsored by Speight's and quite coincidentally, Stephanie's son Josh is on the team.

The relationship between the Stags and Speight's saw the Invercargill Speight's Ale House suddenly become the focus of national media attention when the mighty Southland Stags lifted the Ranfurly Shield from Canterbury in Christchurch on 22 October 2009 – a date that will be firmly etched into the brains of many a Southlander for years to come. The following day the team returned home with the Log o' Wood and headed straight for the Ale House to meet celebrating fans (and the odd slightly dishevelled television presenter!).

While perhaps not as keenly contested as the Ranfurly Shield matches, another contest among the Stags has gained them quite a few fans at the Ale House. Some of the boys have come up with their own burger recipes and they're on the menu on Wednesday nights – it's a hard fought battle between the boys with Jamie Mackintosh, aka Whopper, leading the field with his chicken burger. If you're keen to try out Whopper's recipe, check it out on page 121.

ENJOY THE VIEW.

WE HAVE FOR
OVER 130 YEARS.

SPEIGHT'S AND RUGBY

At Speight's we love our rugby as much as we love making beer.

Speight's first started sponsoring club rugby back in the early 70s and we haven't looked back since. We're now the biggest sponsor of club rugby in New Zealand, supporting local teams from the Deep South to the Far North.

Of course all those club rugby players aspire to representing their province. And it was pretty much the same with Speight's. In 1976, we got behind the Otago rugby team and we've been part of the team ever since. And seeing as Speight's is known as 'the pride of the South' it only seemed right that we sponsor the Southland rugby team as well.

As time went on, we realised that there were good Southern Men all over the country and now we sponsor 13 out of the 26 provincial unions as well as two Super rugby teams.

So here's to all of the supporters and all of the players in all of the teams at all of the clubs and all of the unions that help make rugby the best bloody game in the world.

Good on ya, mate!

WE MAKE 'EM TOUGH DOWN HERE

METHOD	SERVES	MEAT	TIME
PAN FRY	4	**CHICKEN**	**20 MINUTES**

JAMIE MACKINTOSH'S CHICKEN BURGER

Jamie Mackintosh is a man of many talents. Not only is he the Ranfurly Shield-winning captain of the Southland Stags, but he also came up with this recipe for the Invercargill Speight's Ale House, and it's so good they put it on their menu. Is there anything this man can't do?

vegetable oil for frying
4 x 150–180 g chicken breast, schnitzel cut, crumbed
4 hash browns
12 slices streaky bacon
4 large sesame seed buns, cut in half
8 tablespoons mayonnaise
8 tablespoons of your favourite sauce (Jamie recommends a sweet 'n' sour tangy sauce)

4 iceberg lettuce leaves, washed and dried
4 large tomatoes, sliced
200 g cheddar cheese, grated (about 3 tablespoons per burger)
4 pineapple slices, grilled, if that's how you like it
4 long wooden skewers

Method
Preheat the grill to high.

In a large frying pan, pour in enough oil to cover the base. Heat over a moderate heat, then pan fry crumbed chicken breasts. Cook for 5 minutes on each side, remove and place on kitchen paper to drain. Keep warm. (Cut into one a little to ensure they are cooked through – the juices should be clear without any hint of pink.)

Place the hash browns in a shallow roasting dish and grill for 5 minutes each side, until golden brown. Keep warm.

Grill the bacon until crisp, or alternatively pan fry.

Toast the sesame seed buns. Spread 1 tablespoon of mayonnaise and sauce on each of the bun bottoms.

Layer each bun with a lettuce leaf, 3 slices of tomato, a chicken breast, cheese, a hash brown, bacon and a pineapple slice.

Spread 1 tablespoon of mayonnaise and sauce on the each of the bun tops and place on top of the pile. Push a wooden skewer through the middle of each stack to hold it together.

Tip: To turn chicken breast to chicken schnitzel, slip chicken breast into a plastic bag and gently pound it with the flat side of a meat mallet or rolling pin until it is an even thickness. This will ensure the chicken cooks evenly and more quickly.

METHOD	SERVES	MEAT	TIME
BAKE	4	**CHICKEN**	**100 MINUTES**

CHICKEN PARCELS

If a Southern Man is going to get caught eating fruit, he's going to want it to be mixed with meat – these chicken parcels are the perfect combination . . .

3 coriander roots
6 black peppercorns
2 spring onions or shallots, roughly chopped
1 teaspoon salt
4 x 170–180 g chicken breasts
8 rashers streaky bacon, chopped
125 g cream cheese

100 g brie, cut into small pieces
8 dried peaches, soaked in boiling water for 10 minutes, chopped into small pieces
salt and freshly ground black pepper
1 x 375 g packet filo pastry
melted butter for brushing
sesame seeds for sprinkling (optional)

Method

Place coriander roots, peppercorns, spring onions and salt into a medium-sized saucepan. Fill with cold water and bring to the boil over a high heat. Add chicken breasts to the saucepan and stir. Turn off heat and cover with lid.

Leave to poach for about 40 minutes, then remove the lid and allow chicken to cool in the stock. Strain cold stock and refrigerate or freeze for future use.

Preheat the oven to 190°C.

In a non-stick frying pan, lightly fry the bacon.

Soften the cream cheese and add the brie pieces with the chopped peaches. Season with salt and freshly ground black pepper.

Shred chicken and add to cream cheese mixture with the bacon.

To make 1 parcel: place 1 sheet filo pastry on the kitchen bench. Brush lightly with melted butter. Repeat with 3 more sheets of filo. With a sharp knife, cut out 4 corners to remove excess pastry.

Place the chicken mixture down the centre of the filo pastry. Fold over the 2 ends and then fold over sides to form a parcel. Brush with melted butter. Repeat the process to make 3 more parcels.

Transfer parcels to a shallow baking tray, placing seam down. Brush top and sides with melted butter and sprinkle with sesame seeds, if using.

Place in the preheated oven and cook for about 20 minutes until the pastry is golden and crisp.

Tips: If you can't find coriander roots, use 6 parsley stalks instead. Dried peaches are available from bulk bins in supermarkets, or use fresh skinned peaches in season. Serve hot with a salad of rocket and soft herbs dressed with mustard vinaigrette.

METHOD	SERVES	MEAT	TIME
PAN FRY	6	**CHICKEN**	**30 MINUTES**

CROMWELL'S FINEST

Central Otago and apricots – they go together like Speight's and rugby. It's what's called a perfect match.

6 x 180 g chicken breasts
90 g brie
1½ tablespoons sliced almonds, toasted

6 dried Central Otago apricots
salt and freshly ground black pepper
1 tablespoon olive oil

Method
Preheat the oven to 190°C.

With the tip of a sharp knife and starting at the thicker end, make an incision lengthways into each chicken breast to make a pocket.

Cut the brie into 15 g strips, about 6 cm long. Coat each side of brie with almonds. Cut each dried apricot in two pieces and place on top of the brie strips. Insert the almonds, apricots and brie into the pocket cut in the chicken.

Season the chicken.

Heat a large frying pan on a medium to high heat, smear with a little oil. Place the chicken breasts into the pan and lightly brown on both sides.

Place in a shallow oven dish, drizzle over remaining oil and cook for 10 minutes, or until juices run clear.

Serve hot with potato mash and wilted spinach.

METHOD	SERVES	MEAT	TIME
BARBECUE	4	**CHICKEN**	**100 MINUTES**

BARBECUED CHICKEN

Barbies and beer tend to go hand in hand. This beer goes in the chook, but.

1 can Speight's Gold Medal Ale
1 tablespoon sweet chilli sauce
1 tablespoon soy sauce

1 tablespoon oyster sauce
1 whole chicken (1.5–2 kg)

Method
Preheat the barbecue.

Pour half of the beer into a glass.

Mix the three sauces with a splash of the beer out of the glass of beer. Drink the rest of the glass of beer.

Rinse and dry the chicken. Baste the chicken with the sauce mixture and insert the half-full can into the cavity of the chicken. The legs and the can should form a reasonably stable tripod so that the chicken will stand upright.

Stand the chicken on the barbecue plate and lower the barbecue hood. Cook for 1¼–1½ hours, basting regularly so that the skin goes golden brown and crispy. The drumstick should move easily when the chicken is cooked.

Take the whole chicken, can included, off the barbecue and place on a carving board. Let the chicken rest for 5 minutes before removing the beer can – be careful as the can will be hot.

The meat should just about fall off the bone as you carve it.

Tip: The best thing about this recipe is the fun you can have testing it out using all the different Speight's beers. The beer bastes the chicken from the inside out and different beers give different flavours – so feel free to experiment. This is best done on a barbecue with a hood so you can cover the chicken completely and keep the heat in.

METHOD	SERVES	MEAT	TIME
ROAST	4	**CHICKEN**	**1 HOUR**

BLACK CHERRY CHICKEN

Apparently, they cook chicken with lemons up north.
Lemons don't grow down here so we use big, plump, juicy
Central Otago cherries instead.

4 x 180 g skinless chicken breasts
125 g cream cheese
grated zest of 1 orange
freshly ground black pepper
8 rashers streaky bacon
⅓ cup red wine vinegar
2 cloves garlic, crushed

2 tablespoons tomato paste
1 cup red wine (preferably a fruity
    number)
2 tablespoons redcurrant jelly
225 g cherries, pitted
45 g cold butter, cut into cubes
salt

Method

Preheat the oven to 190°C.

With the tip of a sharp knife and starting at the thicker end, make an incision lengthways into each chicken breast to make a pocket.

Soften the cream cheese and mix with the orange zest. Season with freshly ground black pepper. Divide mixture into 4 and spread into the pockets and fold closed.

Wrap each chicken breast well with the bacon. Place in a lightly greased roasting dish and cook for 25–30 minutes. Transfer to a warm plate and keep warm.

Discard excess fat, if any, from the roasting dish and place over a moderate heat. Add vinegar and boil until reduced to 1 tablespoon. Whisk in garlic and tomato paste, then wine and redcurrant jelly. Boil until a syrupy consistency. Stir in cherries and heat them gently.

Remove roasting dish from heat and whisk in cold butter, piece by piece. Season with salt and freshly ground black pepper.

Serve chicken breasts with the cherry sauce and Southern roast veges (see page 234).

Speight's Brewery, Rattray Street, Dunedin, 1905

THE PUSH OF A BUTTON

Most people will do anything to keep a job that they love doing at a place they love working, right? That might be true but there are very few people who will go to the lengths that Fred Button went to in order to keep his job working for Speight's.

Fred Button first started working at the brewery in 1938 and he loved it. Back then, a lot of the beer went out to pubs in wooden casks. The casks themselves were built in the cooperage by specially qualified coopers. New casks would always be stamped with the brewery's name and, so that there was absolutely no confusion, the hoops on the casks would be painted in the brewery's own colours. No one ever had any trouble recognising casks from Speight's as they had bright white hoops on them. The hoops were so recognisable as being from Speight's that the company registered them as a trademark in 1891 – ten years before they bothered to register the name Speight's as a trademark.

Back in the early days, a lot of the wood for the casks was oak imported from Europe. In 1918, some of the coopers were a bit shocked to find bulletholes in the Persian oak that they were working with – until they found out that it had been sourced from Russia while the country was in the throes of a revolution.

The casks that the coopers made would be filled with beer and sent out to pubs. It didn't take long before the casks were emptied by thirsty drinkers. The empty casks would then be returned to the brewery where they were checked, mended if necessary, washed out and used again.

The job of washing out the casks was a huge one. There were 19 men tasked with ensuring that returned casks were spotless and ready to be refilled. One of these men was Fred Button. He spent 11 years cleaning beer casks out by hand before the company invested in the Super Goliath cask washing machine in 1949. The Super Goliath was giant beast of a machine that was almost like a car wash. It sprayed hot jets of water inside the casks while big brushes scrubbed the outside. The machine would then spin the casks to dry them – all at the touch of a button.

That button meant that another Button, Fred to be exact, was out of a job. Well, he was told he was out of a job. But Fred wasn't having a bar of it. He'd worked happily at the brewery for 11 years and he decided that wasn't about to change. Even though he'd been made redundant, Fred just kept on turning up to work. And kept turning up for work. And kept turning up for work. Management tried to explain to Fred that he didn't have a job any more. Fred didn't listen.

In the end, management gave up and offered Fred a temporary job until he found something else. That job turned out to be really temporary – it lasted 27 years!

The brewery carters, c. 1904

The coopers' shop, c.1904

BEER MEASURES

8oz
220 ml

Half pint
260 ml

Pint
520 ml

Jug
1 litre

½ gallon jar (aka
flagon, peter)
2.75 litres

Gallon
1 gallon
4.5 litres

Pin
4.5 gallons
20.25 litres

Firkin
9 gallons
40.5 litres

Kilderkin
18 gallons
81 litres

Barrel
36 gallons
162 litres

Hogshead
54 gallons
243 litres

Butt
108 gallons
486 litres

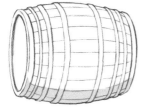

Tun
216 gallons
972 litres

METHOD	SERVES	MEAT	TIME
PAN FRY	4	**FISH**	**40 MINUTES**

SOUTHERN LAKES SALMON

If you're lucky enough to have hauled a decent-sized salmon out of Wakatip, Wanaka or Hawea, then this recipe from Diego Fetter at Cardrona Speight's Ale House, Mount Eden, is sure to do it justice.

500 g orange kumara, peeled and cut
    into even-sized pieces
125 g spinach, stems removed
40 g shaved Parmesan cheese
salt and freshly ground black pepper

2 tablespoons olive oil
4 x 180g salmon portions, skin on and
    boned
4 dessertspoons crème fraîche
2 limes or lemons

Method

Place kumara in a saucepan of salted water and boil for about 15 minutes or until soft. Drain and dry off over the heat. Mash well.

Wash the spinach, allowing any remaining water to cling to the leaves. Heat a medium-sized frying pan.

Place the spinach in the pan without adding more water and cook over a moderate heat, stirring occasionally, for 60–90 seconds or until the spinach has wilted. Set aside in a colander to drain.

Squeeze any excess moisture from the spinach, roughly chop and add to the mashed kumara. Stir in the Parmesan cheese shavings and season with salt and freshly ground black pepper.

Divide the mixture into 4 and shape into cakes or patties.

Heat a frying pan over a low to moderate heat, add 1 tablespoon olive oil and gently fry the kumara cakes until browned on both sides. Watch carefully as they will burn easily. Alternatively, quickly colour the kumara cakes and place on a shallow baking tray lined with baking paper and heat in an oven preheated to 180°C.

Season salmon skin with salt and freshly ground black pepper and rub over the remaining olive oil. Heat a heavy-based frying pan over a high heat.

Sear salmon, skin-side down, for about 3 minutes until golden and crisp,

Reduce the heat to moderate, turn salmon and cook a further 3 minutes until medium–rare.

To serve, place a warm kumara cake on each of 4 warmed serving plates and top with the salmon, skin-side up.

Finish with a spoonful of créme fraîche and half a lime or lemon.

METHOD	SERVES	MEAT	TIME
DEEP FRY	4	**FISH**	**40 MINUTES**

BLUE 'N' GOLD

Back in the day, a couple of Dunedin's founding fathers were tucking in to a feed of blue cod and chips while trying to decide the colours of the Otago rugby jersey . . .

Blue
soya bean oil for deep frying
250 g self-raising flour
½–1 teaspoon turmeric

½ cup Speight's Gold Medal Ale
1 cup cold water
4 blue cod fish fillets or similar
    firm-fleshed white fish

Method
You will need a deep fryer filled to the correct level (sufficient oil so that the fish floats freely) with soya bean oil and preheated to 180°C.

Whisk flour, turmeric, beer and water together until smooth. Add more flour or water if necessary (see tip below).

Dip fish fillets in the batter and carefully place into the deep fryer.

Cook about 5 minutes until golden. They should float to the surface of the oil. Drain on kitchen paper.

Serve hot with golden oven-baked potato wedges (see page 140 and note that if you are serving these together you will need to start the wedges first), coleslaw and tartare sauce.

Pass the salt.

Tip: To test for the correct thickness for the batter, make a figure 8 in the batter and if, by the time you have completed the figure 8, you can still see the start of the figure 8, then you've got it.

Continued over . . .

BLUE 'N' GOLD CONTINUED

Gold

4–6 floury potatoes, such as Agria or
   Ilam Hardy
4–6 tablespoons sunflower oil

1 teaspoon salt
½ teaspoon freshly ground black pepper

Method

Preheat the oven to 190°C. Peel or scrub the potatoes and cut lengthways into even-sized wedges, 8–10 cm long and 4 cm thick.

Bring a saucepan of salted water to the boil and blanch the wedges for 2–3 minutes. Drain the potato wedges well and pat dry with paper towels. Place in a shallow roasting dish.

Whisk together the oil and seasoning. Pour over the top and toss well to coat the potatoes. Place in the preheated oven and cook for 25 minutes until golden brown and cooked through. Shake the potatoes from time to time.

Tips: Blanching potato wedges before roasting will guarantee a crisp wedge that is light and fluffy in the centre, though this step can be omitted.

For a flavour variation add 2 teaspoons cumin and 1 tablespoon coriander seeds to the oil mixture.

SH85 between Ranfurly and Wedderburn

METHOD	SERVES	MEAT	TIME
BAKE	4	**FISH**	**50 MINUTES**

OVEN-BAKED GURNARD

A Southern Man might be surprised to find that you can eat fish if it isn't fried. And his gran might be equally surprised to find rice in a dish that isn't pudding. At Speight's Ale House, Ferrymead, they're full of surprises.

4 x 180 g portions gurnard fillet or
    other white-fleshed fish, such as
    snapper or hapuka/groper
salt and freshly ground black pepper
60 g freshly grated Parmesan cheese,
    extra for serving if desired
250 g asparagus, trimmed and spears
    cut into two or three pieces
2 tablespoons olive oil

50 g unsalted butter
1 small red onion or 4 shallots, finely
    chopped
2 cloves garlic, crushed
1½ cups arborio rice
100 ml white wine
1 litre fish stock, boiling
lemon wedges for serving

Method
Preheat the oven to 190°C.

Season the gurnard fillets with salt and pepper. Place on a lightly buttered shallow baking tray and top with the Parmesan cheese. Set aside while making the risotto.

Blanch the asparagus about 2 minutes until al dente and drain.

Heat the olive oil and half the butter in a heavy-based saucepan over a moderate heat. Add onion and garlic and gently cook about 5 minutes until soft. Add rice and stir until the rice is well coated with the oil.

Reduce heat to low, add the wine and 1 cup of boiling stock and stir for 30 seconds. Allow risotto to cook and the stock to be almost completely absorbed by the rice before adding another cup of stock, then stir again.

Continue adding stock and cooking, stirring frequently, until rice is almost cooked. (It will take 15–20 minutes.)

Place the gurnard in the preheated oven and cook for 7–8 minutes, depending on thickness of fillets.

Add asparagus to risotto and continue cooking until rice is just tender and creamy. Stir in the remaining butter and season with salt and black pepper.

To serve, spoon risotto into 4 warmed shallow bowls, place gurnard on top, and a lemon wedge to the side. Pass the pepper grinder and extra Parmesan cheese, if desired.

KEEP ON TRUCKING . . .

Next time you see a Speight's truck roll past on its way to deliver their fine product to your local pub, bottle store or supermarket, spare a thought for the first Speight's delivery men.

The first 50 years' worth of beer brewed at Speight's was delivered to pubs around Dunedin and parts of Otago by horse-drawn cart. For small local deliveries, a single horse would pull a two-wheeled dray, but for the really thirsty suburbs, a four-wheeled vehicle would be pulled by a pair of horses.

The health and well-being of the horses was vital to the continued supply of beer throughout the region, so while they lived in the stables in the city during the week, the Speight's horses used to spend their weekends grazing fresh grass in the paddocks of Pine Hill.

While they weekended out in the countryside, during the week the horses worked hard. It didn't take long for them to learn their delivery beat and they scarcely needed a driver on board the dray to tell them where to stop – as one poor woman found out. An un-named brewery worker was about to wed his sweetheart and he decided that his bride couldn't possibly arrive at the church on foot. He had a brilliant idea. He hired one of the brewery's horses to draw the carriage carrying his blushing bride to the church for their wedding. It was indeed a gallant move. But, and there's always a but, the plan backfired on the groom somewhat as he was left waiting at the altar. While it might be a bride's prerogative to be late to her wedding, in this case, the bride

couldn't get there soon enough. It was the horse that held her up. Having worked the same route every day of its working life, the smart creature stopped at every pub along the route before it could be persuaded to stop and let the bride out at the church.

It wasn't until 1913 that beer deliveries started to be made by truck but it took a while before the horse-drawn drays were phased out. At the same time as the first company trucks were brought in, Speight's got its first company car. Then, as now, having access to a company car was seen as a bit of a perk. One of the few people who was allowed to drive the car was a salesman called Alf Browne. Even though he was allowed to use the car, Alf would only take it to parts of the region that weren't well served by public transport.

In the city itself, Alf would still visit his city customers on foot. Back in those days, it was a tradition for brewery travellers calling on their customers to shout for the bar. A few canny lads realised that even though Alf could walk fast between calls they could go even faster on their bikes. They worked out Alf's calling pattern and after downing free beer in one pub they'd jump on their bikes and wait for Alf to arrive. They'd get free beer all afternoon and Alf Browne's expense account would get an absolute hiding.

By 1929, the pride of Speight's modernised motor fleet was a brand new Albion with new-fangled pneumatic tyres. The truck was largely used for picking up empty casks and bringing them back to the brewery to be cleaned and refilled. For many years, the Albion was driven by Jack McCartney. As a professional driver, Jack soon earned the nickname Flat-out Jack. This might make it sound like Jack was a man on a mission, racing to get the casks back to the brewery to get them filled and back out to the pubs as soon as possible. Not so! His nickname stemmed from the answer Jack gave whenever anyone asked him if he was busy. 'How's it going, Jack? You busy?' 'Flat out, mate, flat out.'

By the late 1950s, casks were still being sent around the place but really thirsty punters saw the advent of tankers delivering beer around Dunedin. The first Speight's beer tanker held a massive 4773 litres of beer and its first delivery was into the waiting tanks at the Criterion Hotel on Moray Place.

All of which brings us to the present day. There are still a handful of pubs in Dunedin that are supplied by tanker but most of the beer that makes its way into your local bar arrives in kegs, bottles or cans transported by refrigerated beer units – you can't miss them, they've got huge Speight's ads on them and they're a sight for sore eyes. Flat-out Jack, Alf Browne and the boys would be proud.

NO MATTER THE DISTANCE, NOTHING FEELS BETTER THAN DOWNING A COLD SPEIGHT'S WHEN YOU ARRIVE.

METHOD	SERVES	MEAT	STAND	TIME
PAN FRY	6	**VENISON**	**1 HOUR**	**20 MINUTES**

TAIERI VENISON

Whether you've shot it yourself near the banks of the Taieri River, or bought some from a farm on the Taieri Plains, this venison recipe will do your deer justice.

1 kg venison loin
2 tablespoons olive oil
1 teaspoon crushed juniper berries
¼ teaspoon freshly ground black pepper
3 sprigs fresh thyme, leaves picked,
    plus 1 teaspoon chopped fresh
    thyme for sauce

250 ml classic beef jus
½ cinnamon quill
25 g butter, cold and cut into small
    cubes

Method

Rub the venison loin with olive oil, juniper berries, black pepper and whole thyme leaves. Leave to stand for about an hour.

Cut venison loin into even-sized medallions. Heat a large frying pan over a moderate to high heat and cook venison about 4 minutes each side until brown on both sides but still pink in the centre.

Transfer to a plate and keep warm while making the sauce.

In a small saucepan, heat the beef jus with the cinnamon quill until boiling. Remove from the heat and whisk in cold butter, piece by piece. Remove cinnamon quill then stir through chopped thyme.

Serve venison and sauce with potato mash or creamy baked potatoes and a salad of watercress.

Tip: jus is available in plastic pouches in the meat section of most supermarkets. If you can't find any, use beef gravy instead. Juniper berries are found in the spice section of the supermarket.

METHOD	SERVES	MEAT	MARINATE	TIME	
ROAST	4	**VENISON**	**OVERNIGHT**	**2–3 HOURS**	

DENVER LEG

This recipe should come with a warning. It can lead to
spontaneous renditions of the classic Southern Man song,
'Take Me Home, Country Road'.

Venison
1 teaspoon paprika
1 teaspoon ground cumin
1 teaspoon cinnamon
1 teaspoon brown sugar
720 g venison Denver leg
1 tablespoon olive oil

Slow-roasted tomatoes
6 tomatoes, cut in half
1 tablespoon balsamic vinegar
1 teaspoon brown sugar

Potato cakes
750 g potatoes, boiled and mashed
4 tablespoons caramelised onion
2 tablespoons grated havarti cheese
1 tablespoon traditional dukkah
      spice mix
2 egg yolks
flour for crumbing potato cakes
2 lightly beaten eggs for crumbing
      potato cakes
breadcrumbs for crumbing potato cakes
oil for shallow frying

For serving
4 large handfuls watercress
2–3 tablespoons fresh walnuts
Balsamic Dressing (see page 239)

Method
Combine the paprika, cumin, cinnamon and brown sugar on a flat plate. Add the
venison and rub well to coat with the spices. Cover and marinate overnight in the
refrigerator. (Return to room temperature before cooking.)

Now get the tomatoes underway.

Preheat the oven to 130°C. Line a shallow baking tray with baking paper.

Place cut tomatoes on prepared baking tray and sprinkle with vinegar and
sugar. Put in the preheated oven and slow roast for 1–2 hours. Remove from the
oven and set aside.

Start the potato cakes by increasing the oven temperature to 180°C.

Combine the mashed potato with caramelised onion, havarti cheese, dukkah
and egg yolks. Shape into 4 patties, then dust with flour, dip in egg and coat with
breadcrumbs. Cover and chill until ready to fry.

Continued over . . .

DENVER LEG CONTINUED

Heat a frying pan over a high heat. Rub 1 tablespoon olive oil over the marinated venison and brown on all sides. Put in the preheated oven for 8 minutes until medium–rare. Leave to rest covered loosely with foil.

Heat enough oil in a large frying pan to shallow fry the potato cakes. Fry on both sides until golden and hot in the centre.

To serve, slice the venison and place on 4 warmed serving plates with a potato cake each and the slow roasted tomatoes. Serve with watercress and walnuts with Balsamic Dressing.

Tip: To caramelise onions, place 3 or 4 thinly sliced onions in a heavy-based saucepan with 1 tablespoon olive oil and a few leaves of fresh rosemary. Cook over a low heat, covered, until the onion is soft, then remove the lid and continue cooking the onions about 40–45 minutes until they begin to caramelise.

Linnburn Runs Road

METHOD	SERVES	MEAT	MARINATE	TIME
BARBECUE	4	**VENISON**	**15 MINUTES**	**1½ HOURS**

WILD VENISON WITH BEETROOT AND TURNIP SALAD

Gran might have served beetroot in a mysterious jelly, but James Gilbert from Speight's Ale House Palmerston North has gone one better. He roasts it and serves it with wild venison.

Venison
1 tablespoon olive oil
juice of 1 lime
1 teaspoon fish sauce
2 teaspoons manuka honey
1 clove garlic, crushed
1 kiwifruit, peeled and cut into
    small pieces
freshly ground black pepper
2 x 700 g venison denver leg, each
    cut into 4 steaks

Salad
12 baby beetroot
12 baby turnips
2 tablespoons olive oil
2 teaspoons balsamic vinegar
salt and freshly ground pepper
1 tablespoon chopped parsley

Method
In a shallow ceramic or glass bowl, combine 1 tablespoon olive oil, lime juice, fish sauce, honey, garlic, kiwifruit and 1 teaspoon of black pepper. Add the venison, turn over and marinate for 15 minutes.

Preheat the oven to 150°C.

Wash the baby beetroot and turnips. Dry and toss with 1 tablespoon of olive oil and 1 teaspoon of vinegar and season with salt and freshly ground black pepper. Wrap the beetroot and turnips separately in 2 parcels of tin foil and cook in the preheated oven for about 1 hour until tender. Leave to cool, then peel and cut into quarters.

Spoon the remaining olive oil, balsamic vinegar and the chopped parsley over the vegetables and toss to coat.

Remove the venison from marinade and dry with kitchen paper.

Preheat the barbecue hotplate to high heat and cook venison for 1–2 minutes on each side. Alternatively, cook in a hot frying pan.

Serve venison with beetroot and turnip salad, and beef gravy or beef jus, or redcurrant jelly.

HOW TO SPEAK FLUENT BEER

Ale – in medieval England, an ale was brewed without hops, as opposed to a beer that was brewed with hops. Now an ale is a beer brewed with malted barley and top-fermenting yeast. Unlike in the olden days, most modern ales are flavoured with hops.

Ale House – a place to have a couple of quiets and a slap-up meal. An old term for an inn or a pub.

Amber liquid – a peculiarly Kiwi term for beer.

Booze – an informal term for alcohol, from Middle Dutch 'busen', to drink to excess. Could also be derived from the Middle Eastern grain drink, buza.

Bunghole – the hole in a cask that allows the cask's contents to be accessed.

Butt – 1) A 108-gallon cask. 2) Part of the anatomy required to sit on a bar stool at the Ale House.

Draught – a draught beer is generally a beer that has been served from a keg or a tap. If a draught is served from a bottle or a can, it's generally because the brewer has tried to make it taste just like it's come from a keg.

Flagon – *see* half gee/ rigger/peter

Gyles – wooden vats used to ferment beer. The ones at Speight's in Dunedin are made of kauri and kept in good condition with regular applications of beeswax.

Half gee – a half gallon (2.25 litre) container used to take beer home to drink. (See also – peter, rigger)

Handle – a beer glass with a handle on it. Really.

Hops – The bitter seedheads of the hop plant (*Humulus lupus*). Hops were originally added to beer as a preservative but are now added for flavour.

Kettle – The vessel in which a brew of beer is boiled. Made of copper in Speight's Dunedin brewery. Slightly larger than its domestic equivalent.

Lager – In Germany, to lager means to store beer at a cool temperature as the word 'lager' just means storage. The rest of the world knows a lager as a beer that is brewed for a long period at a low temperature using bottom-fermenting yeast.

Pale ale – a beer that is lighter in colour but not in strength. The original pale ale was made by the British for consumption in India. It had a high alcohol content to preserve it on the sea voyage and in the high temperatures of the sub-continent.

Peter – a southern term for the half gee/flagon/rigger, preferably pronounced with a rolling r.

Pilsener – a light lager, named after the town of Pilsen in the Czech Republic where it was first brewed.

Porter – a term first used in London in 1721 to describe a dark beer that was popular with the city's street and river porters.

Quiets, a couple of – one of the best ways to have a Speight's.

Reamer – a tool used for shaping a bunghole.

Rigger – originally a square gin bottle filled with beer. Now used for the modern plastic equivalent of the half gee.

Schooner – a tall beer glass used a lot in Auckland and Australia.

Shout – an endangered Kiwi tradition; when someone else buys the beers.

Skull – a largely Kiwi word for downing the contents of a glass (or bottle) rapidly. Derived from the Scandinavian toast 'skål'. The word skål means 'cup' in several Scandinavian languages. It might have come from the Viking habit of drinking out of their enemy's skulls but only the Vikings can tell . . .

Slab – an Australian term for what Kiwis call 'a coupla dozen'.

Stout – a dark beer that is usually the stoutest or strongest by alcohol content brewed. Stout and porter are closely linked as stout was originally a strong porter and got its name from the strongest 'stout porters' working on the streets of London.

Stubbie – a 330 ml bottle of beer, the consumption of which led to the public wearing of unfashionable shorts of the same name in the 1970s.

X – once used to denote the strength of a beer, although no one knows what strength an X equalled! Speight's Gold Medal Ale used to be known as Speight's XXX. This is thought to have been the origin of the three stars on the beer's label.

The Hawkdun Range

GUARD PACIFIC'S TRIPLE STAR

Speight's Gold Medal Ale was first brewed in Dunedin in 1876. Only way back then it was just called Speight's because it hadn't earned the gold medals yet. Mind you, it only took three years for the beer to start winning awards.

In 1879, a cask of Speight's Strong Ale made its way across the Tasman and won a highly commended award at a beer competition at the international exhibition in Sydney. But the beer's not called Speight's Highly Commended Ale . . .

The following year, Speight's entered four of their beers into another international competition at the Melbourne Exhibition. The fine Dunedin brew was up against tough competition from beers hailing from Great Britain, Europe, the United States and Australia. This time, Speight's tasted sweet, sweet victory, winning two gold medals and four silver medals. But it was those gold medals that mattered most to the boys back in Dunedin. Thus Speight's Gold Medal Ale was born.

As well as featuring the words Gold Medal Ale, the Speight's beer label has also long featured three stars. Those three stars have caused quite a lot of debate over the years on account of a certain line in New Zealand's national anthem. Go on, sing along . . . 'Guard Pacific's triple star . . .' Could it be that the triple star we sing about in our national anthem is the very same three stars that are found on every bottle of Speight's Gold Medal Ale?

The man who wrote those very words was a chap called Thomas Bracken. Now old Thomas was originally from Ireland but he settled in Dunedin in 1869 and lived there until he died in 1898. He very certainly availed himself of Speight's fine product and he even wrote a poem about drinking Speight's at a house-warming party. What's more, he wrote the words to the national anthem in 1876, the same year that Speight's was first brewed . . . Sadly, the three stars on the Speight's label didn't come into being until the 1920s. So there goes that theory.

The words 'Pride of the South' are another feature of the Gold Medal Ale label. Cynics among you might think that this was a slogan thought up by some flash team of advertising executives but that couldn't be further from the truth. In 1980, a competition was held among the staff at Speight's to come up with a new slogan to use in advertising and on the beer. There were plenty of great entries with the winning one being thought up by Jackie Peperkoorn who worked in the office. Jackie's entry was 'Follow the Stars'. So where did 'Pride of the South' come from? Well, it was a painter at the brewery, Malcolm Campbell, who came up with the now famous slogan and his stroke of genius won him second prize and advertising immortality.

DUNEDIN. 593

CITY BREWERY,
DUNEDIN.

JAMES SPEIGHT & CO.,
MALTSTERS & BREWERS.

Report of the Melbourne Jurors.

Messrs Speight and Co. also took First and Second Prizes for their Strong Ales at the Melbourne Exhibition, 1881.—*Vide* Jurors' Report.

"120 barrels of Beer were submitted quite indiscriminately from all parts of the world, and had to be tested against one another at one and the same time.

"Your Jurors have had 11 meetings, extending over a period of one month, from 25th November to 20th December, and have deliberated on an average of thee hours each sitting so that ample time and care was duly taken to form a correct and acceptable judgement.

"W. JOHNSON, Chairman of Jurors."

Christchurch (N.Z.) International Exhibition, 1882.

The Jurors' reports on the Ales are :—

"J. Speight and Co.'s Export Pale Ales.—First-class Ale, and stands out prominently as a very superior Ale. Certificate of Gold Medal."

"J. Speight and Co.'s Strong Ales.—Good sound, Strong Ale of considerable merit. Certificate of Gold Medal."

The Jurors further report :—"Messrs. Speight and Co.'s Ales come to the front, and deserve high commendation, and would attract attention in any competition among that class of Ales —(Signed by the Jurors) J. E. PARKER, W. HOCKLEY, C. ROBERTSON, F. S. HARLEY."

Otago A. and P. Association's Show, 1888.

Heavy Ales.—J. Speight and Co., 1st and 2nd.
Medium Ales.—J. Speight and Co , 1st and 2nd.
Medium Ales.—J. Speight and Co., highly commended.
Light Ales.—J. Speight and Co., 1st and 2nd.
Porter.—J. Speight and Co., 1st.

Glasgow Exhibition, 1888.

A Cask of Ale shown was pronounced by competent experts to be equal to Burton's Pale Ales.

—*Vide* Evening Star, 14th November.

Advertisement, *Evening Star* 14 November 1888

METHOD	SERVES	MEAT	TIME
ROAST	4	**VENISON**	**45 MINUTES**

COUNTRY ROAD VENISON WITH KUMARA HASH

While a leg of lamb is lamb on the bone, a denver leg of venison is boneless meat from the rump of the deer. There, you've learned something today.

Kumara hash
500 g orange kumara, peeled and cut
    into even-sized chunks
2 tablespoons olive oil
salt and freshly ground black pepper
4 rashers streaky bacon, cut into about
    1 cm pieces
2 cloves garlic, crushed
1 sprig rosemary, leaves picked and
    finely chopped

Venison
700–800 g venison denver leg
1 tablespoon olive oil
freshly ground black pepper

Method
Get the kumara organised first. Preheat the oven to 180°C.

Place the kumara in a shallow baking dish, toss with half the oil, salt and freshly ground black pepper. Roast for about 20 minutes until soft. Remove from oven then increase oven temperature to 200°C.

In a small frying pan, fry the bacon until crisp, add the garlic and rosemary and cook for 30 seconds.

In a bowl, lightly smash up the kumara with a fork and add bacon, garlic and rosemary. Divide the mixture into 4 and shape into patties.

Heat the remaining oil in a frying pan and brown the patties on both sides. Transfer to a shallow baking tray lined with baking paper and set aside.

Now get the venison under control. Heat a frying pan over moderate to high heat. Rub the venison with oil and season with freshly ground black pepper. Brown well on all sides, then place in the oven to roast for 8 minutes or until medium–rare. Remove from the oven and cover with foil to rest.

While the meat is resting, warm the kumara hash in the oven.

Serve the venison with kumara hash, broccoli and plum sauce.

METHOD	SERVES	MEAT	TIME
BAKE	4	**VENISON**	**1½ HOURS**

SOUTHERN STAG HOTPOT

Renée Growcott didn't get to be the chef at Speight's Ale House in Invercargill without knowing that Southlanders love two things – their Stags and their swedes.

800 g venison, cut into 2 cm chunks
1 tablespoon olive oil
2 medium onions, finely diced
2 cloves garlic, crushed
2 cups beef stock
115 g butter

1 tablespoon flour
2 teaspoons redcurrant jelly
salt and freshly ground black pepper
1 x 375 g packet filo pastry
800 g Southland swede, cut into chunks

Method
Preheat the oven to 160°C.

Heat a large frying pan over a high heat. Rub the venison with oil and brown on both sides. Do this in batches so as not to overcrowd the pan. Place in a casserole dish.

Lower the heat, add the onion and garlic to the frying pan and cook about 5 minutes until the onion is soft. Add to the venison.

Pour the beef stock into the frying pan, bring to a boil, then pour over the venison. Place in the preheated oven for about 1 hour or until the venison is tender.

Soften 15 g butter and mix with the flour to form a paste and whisk into the venison sauce (whisk in enough so that the sauce is not sloppy). Stir in the redcurrant jelly and taste for seasoning.

Increase the oven temperature to 180°C.

Scrunch up single sheets of filo pastry and place on top of the hotpot.

Melt 50 g butter and brush it over the filo pastry as evenly as possible.

Place in the preheated oven and cook about 20 minutes until the pastry is a good golden colour.

While the hotpot is in the oven, place the swede in a saucepan of salted water and bring to the boil. Boil until tender, about 20 minutes. Dry off over the heat, then mash and stir in the remaining 50 g butter.

Serve the hotpot with the mashed swede and your next-favourite vegetable.

METHOD	SERVES	MEAT	TIME
PAN FRY	4	**VENISON**	**45 MINUTES**

FAIRLIE FEAST

A fair fellow from Fairlie fancied a fine feed. The finest feed the fair fellow could find was a Fairlie Feast. Fair enough.

125 g streaky bacon, cut into pieces
1 onion, finely chopped
500 g mushrooms, finely chopped
salt and freshly ground pepper

1 red capsicum, cored and seeds removed
120 g fresh spinach
4 wild venison steaks
200 ml beef stock

Method
Preheat the oven to 180°C.

In a large frying pan over a moderate heat, cook the bacon until the fat begins to run, then add the onion, mushrooms, salt and freshly ground black pepper. Stir occasionally and cook for about 15 minutes until all the moisture has evaporated. Leave to cool.

Put the red capsicum in a shallow baking dish lined with baking paper and put in the preheated oven and cook until the skin blackens. Remove from oven and leave to cool, before peeling.

Keeping the spinach in its bunches, plunge into boiling water to soften, then refresh in cold water. Leave to drain on kitchen paper before removing stems.

Make a cut in the side of each steak to form a deep pocket. Place in a piece of red capsicum, 1–2 spinach leaves and 1 tablespoon of the mushroom mixture.

Heat a large frying pan with a smearing of oil over a high heat. Cook the steaks on both sides for 4 minutes (2 minutes per side).

Add 200 ml beef stock to the remaining mushrooms and cook until they are hot and the stock reduced until syrupy.

Stir through the remaining spinach.

Serve steaks with the mushroom sauce and a jacket potato or two – or three.

Tip: this stuffing works well in a bone-out shoulder of venison.

METHOD	SERVES	MEAT	MARINATE	TIME
SLOW BRAISE	4	DUCK	AT LEAST AN HOUR	2 HOURS 15 MINUTES

SOUTHERN SPICED DUCK

If you've spent your day freezing your nuggets off in a maimai, a spicy slow braise is the best way to serve the ducks you've brought home.

1–2 teaspoons Cajun seasoning or spice mix
⅓ cup flour
4 duck legs, trimmed of excess fat
1 tablespoon olive oil
1 onion, finely sliced
2 cloves garlic, crushed
1 chorizo sausage, cut into about 1 cm slices
2 large tomatoes, skinned and seeds removed, cut into about 1 cm pieces

1 x 400 g can Roma tomatoes, drained, cores removed and cut into 1 cm pieces
1 red capsicum, cored, seeds removed, sliced
500 ml hot chicken stock
1 bay leaf
salt

Method
On a large flat plate combine the Cajun seasoning and flour. Dust the duck legs with the seasoned flour, rubbing it well into the skin. Leave to stand for at least an hour or overnight, if possible.

Preheat the oven to 150°C.

Heat a frying pan over a low heat and add the oil, onion and garlic. Cook gently for about 5 minutes until the onion is soft. Add the chorizo sausage and cook for 30 seconds. Place in an ovenproof casserole dish with a fitted lid.

Increase the heat to moderate, and brown duck legs on both sides. Transfer to the casserole dish.

Add the fresh tomatoes, canned tomatoes, capsicum, chicken stock and bay leaf and season with salt.

Place in the preheated oven and cook for 2 hours until the meat starts to pull away from the bone.

Serve with potato mash and steamed Brussels sprouts or a salad of rocket leaves with Balsamic Dressing (see page 239).

METHOD	SERVES	MEAT	TIME
GRILL	4	**DUCK**	**40 MINUTES**

DUCK BREAST

When it comes to eating duck, the Southern Man uses his teeth as a metal detector. Unless there's still a bit of shot in there it just isn't fresh enough. If there's not much shot in it, your aim was off.

4 bunches spinach, stems removed
1–2 tablespoons duck fat
700 g floury potatoes, boiled 10–15
    minutes, then cut into chunks
leaves from 1 sprig rosemary

6 garlic cloves, unpeeled
4 duck breasts (about 220 g each)
salt and freshly ground black pepper
250 g classic beef jus
1 teaspoon balsamic drizzle

Method
Preheat the grill to high.

Wash the spinach, allowing any remaining water to cling to the leaves.

Heat a medium-sized frying pan. Place the spinach in the pan without adding more water and cook over a moderate heat, stirring occasionally, for 60–90 seconds until the spinach has wilted. Set aside in a colander to drain.

Heat the duck fat in another large frying pan over moderate heat and add the chunky potatoes with the rosemary leaves and garlic cloves. Toss frequently until the potatoes are a deep gold colour and crusty. (This will take at least 15 minutes of lifting and tossing.)

To prepare the duck breasts, score the fat side with a sharp knife in a crisscross pattern. (This helps to render the fat.) Season with salt and freshly ground black pepper.

Place the duck breast skin-side up and grill for 8 minutes. Pour away any fat from the drip tray (to avoid catching fire), and turn duck breasts. Grill for a further 2 minutes. Transfer duck breasts to a plate and keep warm, allowing them to rest for 5 minutes.

In a small saucepan, heat the classic beef jus and season with salt and freshly ground black pepper. Add 1 teaspoon of balsamic drizzle.

Chop the spinach roughly and add to the potatoes.

To serve, cut the duck breasts into slices and place on 4 warmed serving plates. Place the potato and spinach with garlic cloves and rosemary to the side. Spoon hot jus over the duck breast and a little more balsamic drizzle, if desired.

Tips: Leftover cooked potato is excellent for sautéed potatoes. Sauté potatoes in duck fat, pork fat or oil. The secret is to cook the potato halfway, then drain and sauté with oil or fat and continue to crisp. Use a floury potato such as Agria or Ilam Hardy.

Serve the duck and potatoes with steamed vegetables such as cauliflower, zucchini and carrots or serve simply with green beans.

You can get balsamic drizzle, also known as balsamic glaze, from most supermarkets.

THE MERCY SHIP

Living in the North Island is not without its downside for your average Southern Man. At least, these days, they don't have to worry about going without their favourite drop of the amber nectar. Back in the 1920s though, things were a bit different. And not just because the pub shut at 6pm and you couldn't buy a beer on a Sunday.

Speight's was shipped to the North Island only when the brewery could find space on coastal trading ships so there was no guaranteed supply. A cold Speight's on tap for you at the end of the day was never a certainty.

Now, down in Dunedin, Charles Speight couldn't stand the thought of those poor North Islanders missing out on their favourite brew so he cooked up a plan. He got together with fellow Dunedin businessmen, Richard Hudson, biscuit maker and ancestor of Cookie Bear, and John Shacklock, who probably built your grandma's cooker, and they hatched a plan. They decided that the North Island needed a regular supply of biscuits, beer and ovens.

The first thing they did was go and visit the local head of the Union Company, which ran most of the shipping from Dunedin to the North Island. They asked him very nicely if he could put on a few more boats to help guarantee a supply of their fine products to the hungry, thirsty and stoveless of the North Island. The Union Company chap wasn't to be swayed by the fact that he had representatives of three of the country's largest manufacturers in his office. He pretty much told them that they could put up with the service they got or they could do without all together.

Now, Mr Speight, Mr Hudson and Mr Shacklock weren't the sort of blokes that you said no to. They left the Union Company offices feeling, well, a bit cheesed off. And then they had an idea . . . they'd start their own shipping company.

Along with a couple of good sorts from up north, they set up the Dunedin–Wanganui Shipping Company. Now it's all very well having a shipping company but it's not much use unless you've got a ship. Our wily bunch of chaps realised this and went shopping for a boat that would suit their purposes. They had to go all the way to Ireland to find it, but in the fair city of Dublin they found the *Kylebeg*.

By the time it got to New Zealand, the *Kylebeg* had been renamed the *Holmdale* and the Dunedin–Wanganui Line was in business. By 1922, the *Holmdale* was regularly plying its way up the coast from Dunedin to Wanganui stopping off at Oamaru, Timaru, Lyttelton and Picton. The *Holmdale* was a steamer for many years, and didn't look like the illustration opposite. It wasn't converted to a motorship until 1937.

The arrival of the *Holmdale* assured a regular supply of Speight's to the thirsty souls in the north. It's little wonder that the *Holmdale* wasn't often called by its real name: up north they just knew it as the 'Mercy Ship'.

THE MERCY SHIP – AKA THE HOLMDALE

THE GABLES SPEIGHT'S ALE HOUSE

When it opened in July 2010, the Gables was the northernmost Ale House in the country – but only just as it's only five kilometres away from the Cardrona Ale House in Mount Eden. Now there's a few of you out there that reckon Auckland's Ponsonby is no place for a Speight's Ale House – and you'd be wrong.

It might be the furthest north, but the Gables is an oasis of South in the city. Positioned as it is on Jervois Road, just around the corner from all the fancy bars and cafés of Ponsonby Road, the Gables is the kind of place where any Southerner living in Auckland can go and feel that, just for a little while, they're at home. It's the kind of place you can go and argue heartily over whether cheese rolls should have the crusts on or off and no one will look at you as if you're mad. In fact, you'll even be able to buy a cheese roll as well as heaps of other Southern favourites like seafood chowder, blue cod and chips, and lambs fry with bacon.

The publican at the Gables, Brent Matchett – or Match as he's known to his many friends – is a true Southern Man. He's a good bloke and he knows how to run a great pub. When he's not at the Gables, he spends his time as managing the Auckland emerging players rugby team. It's good of him really, as plenty of those players he's training will end up moving south and taking with them the expertise that Match has passed on.

The Gables' history isn't quite as long as many of the buildings that are home to Speight's Ale Houses but while the building might be short on years, it's been home to plenty of drama. The bar was originally built in the 1970s as an English-style pub. For thirty years, the bar was the hub of the local community but eventually the land it stood on increased massively in value.

In 2006 the Gables was bought by property developers who wanted to demolish the pub and redevelop the site as shops, offices, apartments and a 'gastro-pub'. The pub's regulars and neighbours were less than thrilled at the prospect and mounted a lengthy legal battle against the developers. It took them two years but eventually the locals prevailed.

After a renovation that took about a year, the Gables finally re-opened as a Speight's Ale House on 7 July 2010. Plenty of the neighbours were at the opening night celebrating the part that they had played in retaining their neighbourhood pub.

HE WOULD'VE BEEN QUICKER ON A HORSE.

METHOD	SERVES	MEAT	MARINATE	TIME
ROAST	6	PORK	OVERNIGHT	2 HOURS

PORK BELLY WITH KUMARA GRATIN

This delicious Summit-soaked pork belly should serve six ordinary people or one hungry Southern Man.

Pork belly
2–2½ kg pork belly, bone in and
    rind scored lengthways at 1cm
    intervals
1 x 330 ml bottle Speight's
    Summit beer

Kumara gratin
25 g butter
4 kumara, peeled
1 onion, finely sliced
2 cloves garlic, very thinly sliced
salt and freshly ground black pepper
1 teaspoon flour
500 ml cream, heated

Method
Place the pork belly in a shallow ceramic or glass dish, pour over the beer, cover and marinate overnight in the refrigerator.

Preheat the oven to 180°C.

Line a shallow baking dish with baking paper or tin foil and sit a cake rack on it. Take the pork belly and lay it, rind-side down, on the cake rack and place in the preheated oven.

Roast for 1–1½ hours, then turn the pork belly over and roast for a further 30 minutes until the skin has crackled completely.

About an hour before the pork is going to be ready, grease a deep gratin dish with the butter. Slice kumara thinly and arrange the slices in overlapping rows in prepared dish, adding onion and garlic as you go. Season with salt and freshly ground black pepper.

Mix flour into the cream and pour over the kumara. Bake for 1 hour until the kumara is soft and golden. Keep warm.

Remove pork belly from the oven and use a sharp knife to divide into segments of a few ribs, cutting between the rib bones.

Serve the pork belly with the kumara gratin and a spicy fruit chutney.

METHOD	SERVES	MEAT	MARINATE	TIME
SMOKED/ ROASTED	4	PORK	OVERNIGHT	2 HOURS

SUMMIT-SMOKED WILD PORK

Wiremu Dixon from Speight's Ale House Palmerston North has managed to recreate the flavour of wild pork cooked over a roaring camp fire out in the middle of nowhere in his kitchen in the big city. Cheers, Wiremu.

Smoked pork
1.5 kg pork belly, bones removed, rind on
2 x 330 ml bottles Speight's Summit beer
200 g Darjeeling tea
200 g rice
50 g brown sugar

Rösti
500 g swede, grated
500 g potato, grated
2 eggs, lightly beaten
salt and freshly ground black pepper
1 tablespoon olive oil

Method
To wrangle the pork, put the pork belly into a shallow ceramic or glass dish, pour over the beer, cover and marinate overnight in the refrigerator.

In a smoking tray, mix together the tea, rice and sugar. Put the pork belly on the rack and cover with tin foil. Place over a low-heat flame for 45 minutes. Allow to cool.

Preheat the oven to 180°C.

Put the smoked pork belly in a roasting dish lined with baking paper and roast for 30 minutes.

To prepare the rösti, put grated swede and potato in a tea towel and wring to squeeze out excess moisture, then put into a large bowl. Add eggs and season well with salt and freshly ground black pepper.

Heat oil in a 30 cm frying pan, put in swede mixture and press down with the back of a fork. Cook over a low heat for about 8 minutes then turn the swede and potato cake onto a plate, return it to the hot pan to cook the second side for a further 8 minutes. Transfer to a shallow baking tray lined with baking paper and cook in the preheated oven for 15–20 minutes until the swede is cooked through. (Cover with tin foil if necessary to stop rösti from drying out.) Keep warm.

Preheat the grill to high.

Slice the pork belly into 1cm thick pieces. Grill for about 2 minutes on each side. Keep your eye on it as it will give off a lot of smoke and spit a little. (This can be done on a hot barbecue grill plate.)

Serve the pork belly with wedges of rösti and green peas tossed with a little butter and chopped fresh mint.

Tip: Also good with Apple and Pear Chutney (see page 236).

METHOD	SERVES	MEAT	TIME
STEW	4	HARE	40 MINUTES

WILD HARE STEW

I bet Bryan Ousey from the Speight's Ale House in Palmerston North wishes he had a buck for every time someone says 'Bryan, mate, there's a hare in my stew!'

500 g saddle of wild hare, diced
flour for dusting
1 tablespoon oil
1 onion, finely sliced
4 cloves garlic, crushed

200 ml Speight's Pilsener
250 ml cream of chicken soup
    concentrate
salt and freshly ground black pepper
100 ml cream (optional)

Method
Put the diced hare into a bowl, sprinkle over a little flour and toss to coat.

Heat a large frying pan (with a fitted lid) over a moderate heat and pour in the oil. Brown the hare on both sides and transfer to a plate.

Lower the heat and add the onion and garlic and cook gently about 5 minutes until the onion is soft.

Pour in the beer and allow to bubble up. Add the chicken soup concentrate and season with salt and freshly ground black pepper.

Return the hare to the frying pan, put on the lid and simmer gently for about 30 minutes.

Finish with the cream, if using.

Serve with potato mash and steamed vegetables.

MAINS BEER MATCHING

Arran's
Sore Ribs
– Speight's
Distinction

Rattray
Steak –
Speight's
Old Dark

Shearers'
Shanks –
Speight's
Porter

Grandma's
Lamb's Fry –
Speight's
Old Dark

Highland
Lamb –
Speight's
Distinction

Southern
Man's
Mincemeat –
Speight's Gold
Medal Ale

Jamie Mackintosh's Chicken Burger – Speight's Gold Medal Ale

Chicken Parcels – Speight's Pilsener

Cromwell's Finest – Speight's Summit

Barbecued Chicken – Speight's Gold Medal Ale

Black Cherry Chicken – Speight's Porter

Southern Lakes Salmon – Speight's Summit

MAINS BEER MATCHING

Blue 'n' Gold – Speight's Gold Medal Ale

Oven-Baked Gurnard – Speight's Traverse

Taieri Venison – Speight's Porter

Denver Leg – Speight's Gold Medal Ale

Wild Venison with Beetroot and Turnip Salad – Speight's Porter

Country Road Venison with Kumara Hash – Speight's Old Dark

Southern
Stag Hotpot
– Speight's
Porter

Fairlie Feast –
Speight's Old
Dark

Southern
Spiced Duck
– Speight's
Distinction

Duck Breast
– Speight's
Distinction

Pork Belly
with Kumara
Gratin –
Speight's
Summit

Summit-
Smoked
Wild Pork
– Speight's
Summit

Wild Hare
Stew –
Speight's
Pilsener

The historic Styx Hotel site, Paerau

THE SHEPHERD'S ARMS HOTEL

The Shepherd's Arms Hotel in the Wellington suburb of Thorndon was first built in 1870. While today the hotel stands close to the heart of the city, back in the 1870s it was on the outskirts of the growing town. The hotel's name bears this out as it was called the Shepherd's Arms because its first owners, Charles and Helen Gillespie, thought that the local shepherds from Karori and Makara would trek across the hills to drink there. They were right and the hotel flourished.

When the tram system arrived in Wellington, the Shepherd's Arms Hotel became the terminus for the Thorndon area. The arrival of the trams provided a bonus for the hotel with many thirsty tram passengers popping in for a quiet drink. Whether Tinakori Road's other famous resident, Katherine Mansfield, ever set foot in the hotel is doubtful!

The building itself has changed quite a bit over the years with bits being added and other bits altered. Even the name changed in the 1940s when the Shepherd's Arms became the Western Park. The hotel was incredibly popular with American GIs camped in Wellington.

The Shepherd's Arms underwent its most recent refurbishment in the early years of this century when it became a Speight's Ale House. Its position close to the centre of Wellington but just outside the central business district means it has become a watering hole for many southerners – or northerners who have a rural connection – who have moved to the city for work.

Running the Shepherd's Arms are EJ and Greg. They're welcoming hosts who provide real Southern hospitality, especially when it comes to providing a good yarn along with your meal and drink. The hotel is, they reckon, a great place for Southerners in the city to experience some of the comforts of home.

They're also really proud of their menu. After all, the ale house isn't just about beer. At the Shepherd's Arms – and all the other ale houses – you'll find seasonal, hearty fare. If it's in season, it'll be on the menu – whitebait, duck, oysters . . . you name it. Homesick Southerners almost weep at the sight of blue cod on the menu and Greg heartily recommends their lamb shanks as 'the flashest dog tucker in the world!'

Even the vegetarians are catered for despite the fact that one vege offering almost led to a diplomatic incident. A bunch of blokes from Tokanui in Southland were visiting the big smoke one weekend and after battling the city's one-way road system and being kept awake by all the traffic noise they decided to decamp to the one place they knew they'd be comfortable – the Shepherd's Arms. On arriving, they ordered their beers and inspected the menu. What they found there shocked them. EJ and Greg were summoned and demands were made to remove an item from the menu. That item? The Tokanui Vege Stack. According to the Tokanui lads they don't even have veges in Tokanui!

The Shepherd's Arms Hotel, Tinakori Road, c. 1890s

GENEROUS TO
A FAULT.

Patearoa Paerau Road, Rough Ridge

PUDDING

METHOD	SERVES	SWEET	TIME
BAKE	8	**CHOCOLATE**	**80 MINUTES**

DUNSTAN CHOCOLATE CAKE WITH CHOCOLATE SAUCE

For gold miners up the Dunstan way back when, the thought of a warming tot of whisky at the end of the day was all that kept them going. This cake would have blown their minds.

Cake

⅔ cup cocoa

1 teaspoon vanilla essence

100 ml Glenfiddich whisky

1 cup boiling water

2 eggs

2 cups caster sugar

½ cup sunflower oil

1 cup buttermilk

2 cups plain flour

¼ teaspoon salt

2 teaspoons baking soda

Method

Preheat the oven to 180°C. Line a 23 cm cake tin with baking paper.

In a bowl, whisk together the cocoa, vanilla, whisky and boiling water.

Beat eggs and sugar together until light and fluffy, then beat in sunflower oil. Add buttermilk and hot water mixture.

Sift flour, salt and baking soda into the bowl and beat for a minute or more until shiny. (It will have the consistency of batter.)

Pour into the prepared cake tin and bake for 50–60 minutes or until a skewer inserted into the centre of the cake comes out clean.

Serve with chocolate sauce and ice-cream.

Chocolate sauce

200 g bittersweet chocolate, cut into small pieces

½ cup cream

½ cup milk

1 teaspoon honey

2 tablespoons Glenfiddich whisky (optional)

Method

Combine all ingredients in a small saucepan, including whisky, if using, and heat gently, stirring until smooth.

METHOD	SERVES	SWEET	TIME
BAKE	6	**CREAM**	**2 HOURS**

TRADITIONAL KIWI PAV

Most Southern Men love a big plate of pav at the end of a meal – just don't tell them it's named after a ballet dancer.

4 egg whites

1 cup sugar

1 teaspoon vanilla essence

1 teaspoon malt vinegar

4 tablespoons water

300 ml cream, whipped, for serving

seasonal fresh fruit, chopped, for serving

Method

Preheat the oven to 130–140°C (depending on how hot an oven you have). Line an oven tray with baking paper. Draw an 18 cm circle on the paper.

Place egg whites, sugar, vanilla, vinegar and water in the bowl of an electric mixer and beat on high for 5–10 minutes or until stiff peaks have formed and the mixture is glossy.

Spoon the mixture onto the prepared tray, spreading the mixture to fill the circle as you go. Bake for 1 hour and then turn off the oven and leave the pav in the oven with the door closed to cool.

To serve, spread whipped cream over the top and finish with fresh fruit.

METHOD	SERVES	SWEET	TIME
BAKE	8	**FRUIT**	**1 HOUR**

STICKY DATE PUDDING WITH BROWN SUGAR SAUCE

This is the perfect pudding for those days in winter when you can't see the sun but you can see your breath – even when you're inside with the heater on.

Sticky date pudding
250 g pitted dates
1¼ cups water
1 teaspoon baking soda
125 g unsalted butter
1 cup soft brown sugar

3 eggs
2 cups self-raising flour

For serving:
Brown sugar sauce
4 small bananas
lightly whipped cream or yoghurt

Method
Preheat the oven to 180°C.
    Line a 23 cm cake tin with baking paper.
    Put the dates and water into a saucepan. Bring slowly to the boil and then stir in the baking soda. Set aside to cool slightly.
    Cream the butter and sugar together until light and fluffy.
    Beat in eggs, one at a time.
    Add date mixture. Sift flour into the mixture and fold through. (The mixture will have the consistency of batter.)
    Pour into prepared cake tin and cook for 30–40 minutes or until a skewer inserted into the centre of the cake comes out clean.

Brown sugar sauce
125 g unsalted butter
1 cup brown sugar

1 teaspoon vanilla essence
¾ cup cream

Method
Combine the butter, brown sugar, vanilla and cream in a small saucepan.
    Allow to simmer for 5 minutes before serving with Sticky Date Pudding, sliced banana and whipped cream or yoghurt.
    Makes a good cup.

METHOD	SERVES	SWEET	TIME	CHILL
CHILL	8	**FRUIT**	**40 MINUTES**	**4 HOURS**

CROMWELL CHEESECAKE

There's nothing quite like the taste of a sun-warmed apricot fresh off a Central Otago tree, but this cheesecake is almost as delicious.

Base
1 x 250 g packet wheat digestive
    biscuits
75 g butter, melted
zest and juice of 1 lemon

Filling
250 g cream cheese, softened
¾ cup caster sugar

250 ml cream
1 teaspoon vanilla paste
4 tablespoons water
2 teaspoons powdered gelatine

Topping
1 x 200 g can apricots in juice
1 tablespoon water
1 heaped teaspoon powdered gelatine

Method
Make the base by crushing the biscuits in a food processor and adding the butter, lemon zest and juice.

Press into a 20 cm spring-form cake tin, lined with baking paper if you wish, and chill in the refrigerator.

Make the filling by beating the cream cheese with the caster sugar until smooth. Whip the cream to form soft peaks and fold into the cream cheese with the vanilla paste.

Put the water into a small bowl and sprinkle the gelatine on top. The gelatine will soak up the water like a sponge. Place the bowl with gelatine into a saucepan which has a little boiling water in it and allow the gelatine to dissolve.

Once dissolved, add to the cream cheese mixture and fold well to combine. Pour onto the chilled base and return to the refrigerator.

Next, make the topping by puréeing the apricots with half the juice from the can. Repeat the gelatine process and add to the apricot purée. Pour on top of the cheesecake.

Loosely cover with plastic wrap or use an up-turned plate to cover the cheesecake and place in the refrigerator for at least 4 hours or overnight to set.

Tip: If you are having difficulty finding a jar of vanilla paste, substitute ½–1 teaspoon of vanilla essence mixed with the seeds from 1 vanilla bean. If using gelatine leaves, 2 teaspoons gelatine powder is the equivalent of 4 leaves.

JAMES SPEIGHT

On 6 January 1834 James Speight was born in Bradford, Yorkshire. Speight's father worked as a dyer but James was destined for greater things. After he left school he worked in an office. Despite his prospects in England being quite good, in 1861 James and his wife Mary Jane emigrated to New Zealand. They sailed into Lyttelton but quickly made their way to Dunedin.

Upon arrival in Dunedin, James was employed as an accounts collector but over the ensuing years he followed in his father's footsteps and worked as a dyer. Later he was employed as a clerk, a book-keeper and a salesman. While he was busily changing jobs, Mary Jane was looking after the couple's burgeoning family. James and Mary Jane had eight children, six of whom survived to adulthood.

Fifteen years after arriving in New Zealand, James Speight took a job as a traveller for Well Park Brewery. There he worked alongside Charles Greenslade and William Dawson. It wasn't long before they realised that between the three of them, they had all the skills to run a brewery; Speight was a businessman, Greenslade a maltster and Dawson a brewer.

Together, the three of them began their business by leasing a site for their City Brewery on Rattray Street in Dunedin on 1 May 1876. Naturally, James Speight took charge of the marketing and financial management of the new business – James Speight & Co. Given that the company took his name, James Speight was an ideal candidate to be the company's first chairman. He was also the first licensee of the premises, with his brewing licence granted on 6 June 1876 – two months after the first brew had been made in April!

Not long after the brewing business was established, Speight took out a mortgage and invested in land at Purakanui, north of Dunedin, and in the Catlins to the south. Both of these parcels of land were heavily forested and difficult to access. But Speight was a man of foresight – when roads made the two areas accessible, he had the trees felled and ferried the wood back to the city where it was sold at a profit for firewood.

Despite being the licensee, the chairman of the board and the marketing guru for the company, James Speight spent surprisingly little time in his office. Instead, he was out on the road selling the company's product. Speight had the winning combination of the gift of the gab and a fine product to sell so the company grew quickly.

A mere 11 years after he founded the company, James Speight passed away. He was only 53 years old. His wife Mary Jane took his place in the partnership while Charles Greenslade took over as company chairman. But a second generation of Speights was now working at the brewery as James and Mary Jane's son Charles had started working there in 1881 and would eventually take his turn as board chairman. In years to come, Charles' son Hugh would also helm the company ensuring the continuation of the Speight name within the brewery.

James Speight, mid 1880s

CHARLES GREENSLADE

Born in 1843 in Devon, Charles Greenslade grew up in the villages of Thorverton and Crediton. On leaving school he got a job working for a grain merchant and it was while working there that he learnt his trade as a maltster and miller. English beer clearly wasn't enough of a challenge for the young man as at the age of 20 he emigrated to New Zealand, landing in Bluff in 1863.

He didn't take up a brewery job straight away when he arrived here but first tried to earn a living as a carrier and then headed for the goldfields of Central Otago. After 18 months of trying to eke a living out of the hard Otago soil, Greenslade decided to try his luck under the bright lights of Dunedin. It took him a while to get there as he kept running out of money and having to take temporary jobs. When he eventually made it to the city he got a job working as a miller at Seimetz Bakery.

Having attained gainful employment, Greenslade courted and married Caroline Mason. The couple then moved to Waikouaiti for a brief period where Charles continued to work as a miller. The lure of the malt drew him back to Dunedin in 1868 when he became the maltster for the Red Lion Brewery (no relation of the Lion Red we know today) and then at the Well Park Brewery where he met William Dawson and James Speight.

While the trio's new company eventually flourished, in the early years things were a little tight with Greenslade

sometimes struggling to put food on the table for his family. It wasn't until the brewery's success at the international exhibition in Sydney in 1879 that things really started to pick up.

Before too long the Greenslades were living in a magnificent home in Tennyson Street and retiring to their holiday home, Burkes, on the banks of Otago Harbour when they needed a rest from the hustle and bustle of city life. Charles Greenslade was, after all, the chairman of the largest brewery in New Zealand. He deserved some of the trappings of his success.

As the years drew on, William Dawson became more involved in civic matters while Greenslade was more focused on the brewery. Despite this, the two men remained close, as they were both very active members of the Caledonian Bowling Club and they would regularly head north to Hanmer Springs together to soak in the hot springs thereby relieving the arthritis they both suffered from.

Apart from his healthful jaunts north with William Dawson, Greenslade only once returned to visit the country of his birth. He was well and truly a Dunedin man and he was happy to stay put in Otago and carry on working. So dedicated was Charles Greenslade, he died in his office at the brewery on 19 October 1917 at the age of 74. As was company practice, Greenslade's son Bob was working for the brewery and filled his father's place on the board.

Charles Greenslade, mid 1880s

WILLIAM DAWSON

In January 1852, William Dawson was born in the Scottish city of Aberdeen. From his first days he practically had beer in his veins as his father – also named William – was a brewer. In young William's early years, the family moved around spending time in Montrose and then in Durham. School never held much attraction for the young Scotsman who soon learned the art of making beer from his father.

At the age 21, William Dawson emigrated to New Zealand arriving in Port Chalmers on 2 July 1873. Little did he know that he was going to make quite a mark on his new home in nearby Dunedin. It didn't take him long to find employment as a brewer and he was soon working alongside James Speight and Charles Greenslade at James Wilson's Well Park Brewery.

William was the first brewer at the City Brewery of James Speight & Co when the three men went into partnership in 1876. Another partnership soon followed when Dawson married Mary Ann Andrews a couple of years later – the couple had four daughters and two sons.

In the early years at the brewery, Dawson worked hard doing most of the brewing himself. It is largely down to his skill as a brewer and his willingness to experiment with recipes that gained Speight's its early successes in international competitions. Despite his young age, Dawson's years of experience made him a real asset to the company.

Success meant that Dawson and his wife, Mary Ann and their children could move into their grand new home in Duncan Street up the hill behind the brewery. The house tracked Dawson's successes over the years, becoming gradually grander with a series of spectacular renovations and expansions.

It wasn't just the Dawson home that became more grand through the years. In 1885 William Dawson was elected to the Dunedin City Council. He served the city so well that in two years' time he became the city's mayor. He was only 35 years old and he remains one of the city's youngest ever mayors.

While Dawson pursued his political career, the brewery was in the safe hands of the Speights and the Greenslades – and eventually, his own son, Reginald. Knowing that the brewery was flourishing, Dawson was happy to stand for parliament in 1890. He was duly elected and represented Dunedin suburbs at the House of Representatives in Wellington. While in parliament, Dawson used what influence he had to try and ensure that prohibition didn't occur.

As if being an MP and a director of a brewery wasn't enough, Dawson owned a jewellery store, represented Dunedin on the Otago Harbour Board and was president of the New Zealand Bowling Association as well as the Caledonian Bowling Club and Otago Bowling Club (which was established in 1906 on his own property). He also donated much of the money required to build Otago Medical School.

When William Dawson died on 27 July 1923, he was the last of the brewery's founders to pass away.

William Dawson, mid 1880s

METHOD	SERVES	SWEET	TIME	
BAKE	8	**FRUIT**	**1½ HOURS**	

ROXBURGH RHUBARB CAKE

It's a little known fact that it's illegal not to have a rhubarb plant in your garden in Southland. This cake is so good it should probably be illegal too.

Cake
125 g butter
1¾ cups soft brown sugar
2 eggs, lightly beaten
1 teaspoon vanilla essence
grated zest of 1 orange or lemon
250 g sour cream

2½ cups flour
1 teaspoon baking soda
1 teaspoon cinnamon
500 g rhubarb, cut into 1 cm pieces

Topping
1 tablespoon soft brown sugar
1 teaspoon cinnamon

Method
Preheat the oven to 160°C. Line a 22 cm cake tin with baking paper.
    With an electric mixer cream the butter and sugar together until light and fluffy.
    Add the eggs, beating well. Stir in the vanilla and orange zest. Fold in the sour cream.
    Sift together the flour, soda and cinnamon and fold through the creamed mixture.
    Lastly fold through the rhubarb pieces. Spoon mixture into the prepared cake tin.
    Make the topping by mixing the soft brown sugar and cinnamon together. Sprinkle on top of the cake mix. Bake for 1 hour or until a skewer inserted in the centre of the cake comes out clean.
    Leave for 10 minutes before removing from the tin.

METHOD	SERVES	SWEET	TIME
BAKE	8	**CHOCOLATE**	**75 MINUTES**

WHITE CHOCOLATE MUD CAKE WITH RASPBERRY SAUCE

Serve a Southern Man a dark chocolate mud cake and he'll take it outside and compare the colour and consistency with the stuff on his truck tyres. Serve him white chocolate mud cake and he'll just eat it.

Cake
250 g butter
1 cup sugar
250 white chocolate
200 ml water

2 eggs
½ cup sour cream
½ teaspoon vanilla essence
2½–3 cups flour
1½ teaspoons baking powder
icing sugar for dusting

Method
Preheat the oven to 180°C. Line a 21 cm cake tin with baking paper.

Put butter, sugar, white chocolate and water into a saucepan and gently melt.

Mix eggs, sour cream and vanilla together. Stir into the melted butter mix. Sift in the flour and baking powder and mix well.

Pour mixture into tin and bake for about an hour or until a skewer comes out clean.

Serve warm, sprinkled with icing sugar, with whipped cream, Raspberry Sauce and raspberries, if it's the season.

Raspberry sauce
250 g raspberries

juice of 1 lemon
½ cup icing sugar

Method
Blend ingredients in a food processor until shiny. Press through a sieve to extract raspberry seeds.

Taste for sweetness and add more sugar, if necessary.

Makes 1 cup.

METHOD	SERVES	SWEET	TIME
BAKE	4	**FRUIT**	**40 MINUTES**

SOUTHERN CRUMBLE

If there's one recipe that can make a Southern Man go a bit teary-eyed, it's his mum's apple crumble. If she won't part with her recipe, try this one. Like Mum does, serve hot with vanilla custard.

Fruit
600 g or 3–4 large apples, peeled
    and cored
2 cloves
¼ piece of cinnamon quill
¼ cup sugar (use vanilla sugar
    if available)
¼ cup water
150 g blueberries

Crumble
1 cup flour
½ cup soft brown sugar
75 g cold butter, cut into small
    even-sized pieces
70 g toasted hazelnuts

Method
Preheat the oven to 180°C.

Slice the apples and place in a saucepan with the spices, sugar and water. Bring to the boil, cover, then lower the heat to a simmer and cook gently for 10 minutes. Remove the spices then add the blueberries and set aside.

Place the flour and sugar for the crumble topping in a bowl and rub in the butter until the mixture resembles coarse breadcrumbs. Roughly chop the toasted hazelnuts and add to the mixture.

Put the apple and blueberry mixture into a 4-cup capacity ovenproof dish. Sprinkle the crumble topping over the fruit and bake for 20 minutes until the crumble is golden.

Tips: Nuts are toasted to bring out their flavour. Spread hazelnuts on a baking tray and toast at 160°C for about 10 minutes. Check and shake the tray so the nuts toast evenly. Place hazelnuts in a clean tea towel and rub to remove as much skin as possible. Discard skins.

To make vanilla sugar: bury some vanilla beans in a jar of caster sugar and the sugar will become perfumed.

METHOD	SERVES	SWEET	TIME	CHILL
FREEZE	8	**CREAM**	**4 HOURS**	**OVERNIGHT**

SPEIGHT'S 5-MALT ICE-CREAM

Speight's Old Dark is a 5-malt beer. This is a 5-malt ice-cream. You do the maths. You'll need to hunt down some Maltexo – it's a mix used to make homebrew beer taste malty. You should find it at supermarkets and in some liquor stores, and in Nana's pantry as a treat for the grandkids.

1 cup milk
2 cups cream
1 vanilla bean, split to release seeds,
    or 1 teaspoon vanilla essence

6 egg yolks
½ cup sugar
1 cup Maltexo

Method

Put the milk, cream and split vanilla bean into a saucepan and heat until warm.

In a bowl, using a wooden spoon, beat together the egg yolks and sugar then pour on the warm milk mixture.

Wipe out the saucepan and return the mixture to the pan. Cook over a low heat until the custard thickens and coats the back of a wooden spoon. Do not allow the mixture to boil or it will curdle. Remove from the heat and stir in the Maltexo. Cover the surface of the custard with baking paper and leave to cool.

Churn in an ice-cream machine according to manufacturer's instructions. Alternatively, pour the mixture into a plastic or stainless steel pan and place in the freezer. After 45 minutes, remove the pan from the freezer and stir the mixture vigorously to create the smoothest texture possible. Return the pan to the freezer.

Every 30 minutes, repeat this stirring to minimise the formation of ice crystals while the ice-cream freezes. After about 2–3 hours the ice-cream will be frozen, but it's best left overnight. Store in a sealed container suitable for the freezer.

Tips: You can freeze the egg whites to use to make a pav.

You can add a variety of toppings like roasted nuts or chocolate shavings to this delicious ice-cream.

METHOD	SERVES	SWEET	TIME
BAKE	6	**BISCUITS**	**20 MINUTES**

TODD'S GRANNY'S KISSES

A Southern Man may not get emotional often, but when it comes to his granny he can get a little soft . . .

125 g butter
125 g sugar
2 medium eggs
125 g flour
100 g cornflour

1 teaspoon cream of tartar
½ teaspoon baking soda
6 tablespoons raspberry jam
icing sugar for dusting (optional)

Method
Preheat the oven to 190°C. Line a baking tray with baking paper.

With an electric mixer cream the butter and sugar. Add eggs and then the sifted dry ingredients.

Using a small dessertspoon, place mixture on prepared tray and bake for 10–12 minutes until golden.

When cooked, remove from tray and place on wire rack to cool.

When cold, stick pairs of kisses together with raspberry jam and sprinkle with icing sugar, if desired.

Makes 12 double biscuits.

Linnburn Runs Road, Rock and Pillar Range

PUDDING BEER MATCHING

Dunstan Whisky
Chocolate Cake
with Chocolate
Sauce – Speight's
Old Dark

Traditional
Kiwi Pav
– Speight's
Summit

Sticky Date
Pudding –
Speight's
Porter

Cromwell
Cheesecake
– Speight's
Pilsener

Roxburgh
Rhubarb Cake
– Speight's
Gold Medal
Ale

White
Chocolate
Mud Cake
with Raspberry
Sauce –
Speight's Porter

Southern
Crumble –
Speight's
Porter

Speight's 5-Malt
Ice-cream –
Speight's
Old Dark

Todd's
Granny's
Kisses –
Speight's
Pilsener

IF YOU CAN'T TAKE
~YOUR MATE~
TO THE PUB

TAKE THE PUB TO YOUR MATE

It began with Tim, a good Kiwi lad in London missing his Speight's, and his mates. He told us about his problem. Something had to be done, he was a mate in need. So we set about sending him over a few dozen. But before it was sent, the question had to be asked: "How many Kiwis in London are also missing their Speight's?" It turned out there were plenty and a few dozen weren't going to do the job. Then, over a few cold Speight's, someone had the crazy idea of sending over an entire pub. "Can't be that hard, we've moved pubs before," someone added.

So it was decided to send a Speight's Pub over to London. James (Tim's best mate) said he'd go. Good on ya mate. We found a boat and all that was needed then was a crew. 2000 people applied for the vacant crew positions. Over a few Speight's, four keen lads were picked. Jamie, Tim C, Mark and Lindsay. The Great Beer Delivery could begin.

{07/09/2007} A pod of whales passes only 5 metres off the starboard side of the boat. Must have known Speight's was on board.

DUNEDIN
25/07/2007

{25/07/2007} The boat left Dunedin with a crowd of waving onlookers and bagpipes playing. The boys looked back at New Zealand. It was going to be two weeks until they saw land again and three months before they reached London.

{03/09/2007} Each year more then 14,000 ships pass through the canal, but only 1 has had a fully functional, working, Speight's Pub on board.

PANAMA
31/08/2007

Loading precious cargo... she's a beauty and the boat is not so bad herself.

{29/07/2007} A 15 metre wave smashed the boat! The violent rocking flicked on the Speight's taps in the bar. Speight's flooded the floor. What a waste of the fine golden nectar. A tear or two were shed by the boys.

{02/09/2007} Unfortunately due to family commitments Lindsay makes the hard decision to leave the boat here and fly back to Dunedin. He was sorely missed.

{01/08/2007} Having a few quiet ones down in the bar.

{02/08/2007} The guys enjoying a slap-up meal. Looking forward to Samoa.

{29/08/2007} After being at sea alone for 3 weeks, the boys get stuck in the world's biggest shipping log jam.

SAMOA
04/08/2007

{06/08/2007} The boys show off some mean dance moves or were their sea legs playing up?

{05/08/2007} A new Captain comes on board. He sets a strict policy on board. "If you are sick and you don't work, then you can't eat." Sweet as, we have heaps of Speight's anyway.

{07/08/2007} Word spread of the arrival of the Speight's Pub. Rude not to have a few with a bunch of thirsty ex-pat Kiwis.

{08/08/2007} The boys played touch against a Samoan rugby team. Ah... Rugby was the winner on the day and a few cold Speight's were shared.

{12/08/2007} MV Lida stops to cross the equator at 12.30pm (ship time). Ship crew and Neptune put the lads through their initiation.

{09/2007} New Mulligan from 'The Crowd Goes Wild' joins the crusade to get the pub to the Speight's to London. Quite the picnic he thought it was going to be. A bit soft we reckon.

{10/09/2007} Steve Nichols arrives to replace Lindsay and instantly shows some southern hospitality sharing some Speight's with some thirsty locals.

{16/09/2007} "Do you think she'd like a Speight's?" "Silly question, course she would".

FROM **DUNEDIN** TO **LONDON**
"FOR A MATE"
SPEIGHT'S
THE **GREAT BEER DELIVERY**

Pride of the South

BAHAMAS
09/09/2007

{10/09/2007} The boys head to Stuart Cove to go sub-diving and snorkelling. Taking in a bit of James Bond action.

NEW YORK
16/09/2007

{20/09/2007} The boys hook up with Steve Williams for some golf tips, in exchange for a few Speight's of course.

{07/09/2007} Using a 40 gallon drum, Mark uses a bit of Kiwi ingenuity to make a BBQ.

{21/09/2007} New York welcomes the Pride of the South. The first pint of Speight's is poured at the Kiwi bar, Nelson Blue. Good on ya mates.

{01/10/2007} Smack bang in the middle of a massive storm. The boys use extra rope to tie down the precious cargo of Speight's. So close now, to lose the kegs overboard would be heartbreaking.

{27/09/2007} "Seen the movie A Perfect Storm?" is how the Captain describes the upcoming last leg of their journey. "It's going to get rough".

POSSIBLE TROPICAL CYCLONE FORMATION NEXT 48 HOURS

{01/09/2007} Lindsay shows great Southern Man hospitality by gifting some precious Tri-Star to the canal workers. "They did a good job," said the laconic mid-Cantabrian.

{12/08/2007} The boys launch the Speight's keg raft, unfortunately it ends up going under the Equator rather than over it.

LONDON
08/10/2007

{08/10/2007} Three months and 34,779kms down, the fully operational Speight's Pub sails up the river Thames. The boys have done it!

THE PUB ARRIVES IN LONDON

IT'S TIME FOR A BEER WE RECKON

Tim was waiting at the port. Finally his Speight's had arrived.
James poured him a cold one and they sat at the bar and
exchanged a few yarns. What better way to end a journey to help
a mate, than over a few cold Speight's.

RADIO **SPORT** Just Sport

SPEIGHT'S CRAFT RANGE

The three brews in the Speight's Craft Range – Distinction Ale, Porter and Pilsener – were originated from recipes of a bygone era in a quest to recreate flavours as true as possible to the original styles.

Two of the Craft Range brews, Porter and Pilsener, are fermented in kauri gyles: open-topped wooden fermentation vats which are lined with beeswax. Small volume and labour intensive, these open, shallow vessels help to bring out the seamless character and full aromas of the brews. Only one other brewery in the world is still known to use kauri gyles.

Speight's Distinction Ale

Speight's Distinction was first brewed to celebrate Speight's 118th birthday in 1994. It was meant to be a temporary addition to the Speight's stable of beers but it was so popular production has continued ever since.

Beer style: Traditional dark ale

Based on: A strong ale first brewed by Speight's in the 1880s

First brewed: 1994

Colour: Red-brown

Flavour characteristics: Speight's Distinction Ale is a full-flavoured malt ale. Five malts have been blended to create this premium ale's full malty bitterness. The predominant impression is of caramel and butterscotch flavours with a light hoppy note, providing a clean, extended finish.

Food match: The full flavour of this ale is not intimidated by big red meat dishes and it holds its own against casseroles, steaks and venison.

Speight's Porter

A Porter is a dark beer something akin to a stout. The dark brew became a firm favourite with London's street porters – the forebears of present-day bike couriers – during the eighteenth century. In fact, the porters liked it so much, the beer ended up being named after them.

Beer style: Porter

Based on: 1929 Speight's double malt stout recipe

First brewed: 2002

Colour: Red-black

Flavour characteristics: Speight's Porter has a rich, robust palate and complex full aromas. A blend of crystal, caramalt, roasted wheat and chocolate malt combine to give a complex, smoky, mocha aroma and a rich coffee flavour which finishes on a subtle chocolate note.

Food match: Porter is a brilliant match with strong flavours like blue cheese. Harking back to its London roots, it is also traditionally matched with oysters. With its chocolate malt, Porter is good matched with chocolate dessert.

Speight's Pilsener

Speight's first produced a Pilsener in 1955. This pale lager takes its name from the Czech city of Pilsen where it was first brewed in by Josef Groll in 1842.

Beer style: Pilsener

Based on: 1955 recipe for Speight's Pilsener

First brewed: 2002

Colour: pale straw

Flavour characteristics: Hoppy, bitter, clean and crisp. With such a classic Czech lager style, the challenge is to achieve flavour balance between characterful malts and the strong hop content. Nelson Sauvin and New Zealand Saaz hops are added at boil's end for a fresher fruitier aroma. The biscuit residual sweetness of Munich malt provides the balance, leaving a clean finish.

Food match: Great with any spicy food dishes, particularly Indian and Thai cuisine. It's also a great match with rich and creamy food as it cuts through the cream nicely.

Copper brew kettles, Speight's Brewery, Dunedin

THE BREWERY TAP

Ever since the early days of Speight's, the brewery has used water from a spring that lies directly below the brewery. So that everyone could share the goodness, the brewery installed a tap in the side of the Rattray Street building so that the public can have access to some of the freshest, purest water anywhere.

On 1 April 1998, the *Otago Daily Times* did what it does best – they ran a cracking April Fools' Day joke on the front page of the paper. In an article entitled, 'Celebratory offer of free beer should go down well,' they claimed that the Speight's tap would be pouring a new beer, 'In the Dark Ale', until noon that day.

Now you'd think that your average Southerner would be smart enough to see through such a prank but, sadly for them, there were plenty who didn't look closely at the day's date before loading up the car with every empty vessel they could find and heading for the brewery.

Whether it was their love of Speight's or the chance for some free beer, there were plenty of locals sucked in by the story. While they didn't get the promised beer, they could still fill up their flagons with delicious pure Speight's water.

Since then, Speight's have used the spring water as a source of revenue for the Speight's Brewery Environment Fund. The fund was established in 2009 and is designed to support not-for-profit groups supporting Dunedin's natural environment. The brewery donates $25,000 to the fund each year and this is topped up with donations from people who take water from the brewery tap.

While payment for the spring water is not compulsory, the brewery asks people who use the tap to donate ten cents for each litre that they take. That money then goes into the environment fund. Money for the fund also comes from the sale of reuseable water bottles from the visitor's centre.

The fund's first three grants were made in 2009. The Dunedin Royal Forest and Bird Protection Society received funding towards re-establishing seabird colonies on the cliffs at St Clair and Long Point. A group working towards restoring Hawksbury Lagoon near Waikouaiti also received a grant for 3500 raupo to be planted around the lagoon. The third grant went to Orokonui Ecosanctuary for continued work establishing a mainland sanctuary for rare and endangered flora and fauna, including takahe, kaka, saddlebacks and jewelled geckos.

Speight's Brewery, Dunedin, 2006

AT SPEIGHT'S WE KNOW
A THING OR TWO ABOUT
MAKING THINGS THAT
ARE LEGENDARY.

Vulcan Hotel, St Bathans, Central Otago

Laws Road, near Wedderburn

ACCOMPANIMENTS

THE ALE HOUSE LOAF

This is delicious served with hot soup or made into sandwiches with leftover roast meat – if there is any.

2¼ cups wholewheat flour
1 tablespoon sugar
1 tablespoon baking powder
½ teaspoon baking soda
¼ teaspoon salt

½ 330 ml bottle Speight's Distinction beer, or more if needed to make a stiff batter
2 tablespoons olive oil

Method
Preheat the oven to 190°C. Line a 4-cup capacity loaf tin with baking paper.

In a large bowl, combine flour, sugar, baking powder, baking soda and salt. Make a well in the centre. Pour in beer and olive oil and mix until just blended.

Pour batter into prepared loaf tin and bake 30–35 minutes, or until a skewer inserted in the centre comes out clean.

Tip: For a herbed loaf add 1 tablespoon of chopped herbs such as thyme, parsley, basil, oregano.

Cuts into 8–10 slices

BEER BREAD

This is a real beginner's bread recipe. The resulting loaf has a lovely beer flavour. And who isn't partial to that?

¼ cup warm water
1 package active dry yeast
1 cup beer, at room temperature
1 tablespoon cream cheese, softened

1 tablespoon sugar
1–1½ teaspoons salt
3 cups white flour, sifted

Method
In a small bowl mix the water and yeast. Stir gently until the yeast has dissolved.

Pour the beer into a large bowl and add cream cheese, sugar and salt. Pour in the yeast and 2½ cups of flour. Mix to form a lump-free dough ball.

With the remaining flour, flour a bench top and turn out the dough onto it. Knead the dough about 10–15 minutes until it is soft and smooth.

Put dough into a lightly oiled large bowl, turn the dough over to prevent a skin forming, cover and leave to rise in a warm place for about 1 hour or until the dough has doubled in size.

Preheat the oven to 190°C. Lightly oil a standard loaf tin.

Punch dough down and form into 1 loaf. Place in prepared tin, cover and leave to rise 20–30 minutes until it reaches to the top of the tin. Make 3 cuts with a sharp knife across the top of the dough and bake for about 45 minutes until golden.

Turn the bread out and tap the bottom: if there is a hollow sound then the bread is cooked.

Leave to cool on a wire rack.

Makes 1 loaf

SOUTHERN ROAST VEGES

This recipe is easy and delicious. It can only be improved by adding a big plate of roast meat.

4 medium potatoes (about 750 g)

2 onions, peeled, leaving root intact, and cut into wedges

3 cups peeled and evenly cut vegetables, such as pumpkin, swede, parsnip and carrot

2 tablespoons oil

2 tablespoons rosemary leaves

1 teaspoon chicken stock powder

salt and freshly ground black pepper

Method

Preheat the oven to 180°C.

Place the vegetables in a large roasting dish. Drizzle over the oil, rosemary leaves, stock powder and season with salt and freshly ground black pepper.

Toss well to coat vegetables with oil and seasonings. Roast vegetables for 40 minutes or until soft and golden.

Serves 4

MASHED POTATO

Really good mashed potato goes with everything. Make plenty.

3 large floury potatoes, such as Agria or Red Rascals, peeled and cut into even-sized pieces

1 teaspoon salt

⅓ cup hot milk or a mixture of milk and cream

25 g butter

Method

Put potatoes in a large saucepan and cover with water, add salt and boil about 20 minutes until tender.

Drain, then dry off over the heat, shaking the saucepan, until the potatoes appear dry.

Mash the potatoes then, using a wooden spoon, beat in the hot milk, then the butter until light and fluffy.

Variations: For garlic mash add about 6 cloves of roasted garlic.

For Dijon mash add about 3 teaspoons Dijon mustard to the milk and beat into the potato.

Serves 4

BEETROOT RELISH

This is great in sandwiches. It's also good on the side, with cold meat or chicken.

1 tablespoon olive oil
2 onions, finely sliced
1 kg beetroot, peeled and grated
100 ml white-wine or red-wine vinegar
1 tablespoon brown sugar

2 tablespoons mustard seeds
1 bay leaf
2 sprigs thyme
salt and freshly ground black pepper

Method
Put the oil and onions into a large saucepan. Cook slowly about 10 minutes until soft.
　　Add the beetroot, stir well and cook for 5 minutes. Add the vinegar, sugar, mustard seeds and herbs. Season well with salt and freshly ground black pepper.
　　Simmer over a low heat, covered, for 1 hour or until the beetroot is soft. Stir from time to time.
　　About 15 minutes before the end of cooking, remove the lid and allow most of the liquid to evaporate.
　　Leave to cool, then put into clean jars and refrigerate. Keeps for 2 weeks.
　　Makes 4 cups

HUMMUS

The perfect recipe for a Southern Man who wants to impress a Northern Lady . . .

2 x 400 g cans chickpeas (2 cups), well
　rinsed and drained
4 teaspoons tahini
2 cloves garlic, crushed

½ teaspoon toasted cumin seeds, ground
juice of 1 lemon
½ cup olive oil (more or less)
salt

Method
Put the chickpeas, tahini, garlic, cumin and lemon juice in the bowl of a food processor. Process until smooth. With the motor purring, drizzle in the olive oil to make a soft purée. Season with salt.
　　Makes 2 cups

BLACK CHERRY CHUTNEY

This chutney is lovely and rich. It's perfect with venison or beef.

1 tablespoon oil
1 small onion, finely diced
1 x 300 ml jar black or sour cherries,
    pitted, in juice
50 g brown sugar

2 whole cloves
2 star anise
2 cm piece cinnamon quill
50 g currants

Method
Put the oil and onion in a small saucepan and cook over a low heat until the onion is soft, about 10 minutes. Add the cherries with the juice and brown sugar.
    Wrap the spices in a muslin cloth and add to the saucepan.
    Simmer for about 30 minutes until the juice has been absorbed. After 15 minutes add the currants.
    Leave to cool before refrigerating. Will keep for about one week.
    Makes 1¼ cups

APPLE AND PEAR CHUTNEY

Most people think of chutneys the way squirrels think of nuts, but this chutney only keeps for a week, if it gets the chance. It's tasty with cheese in a sandwich or with any cold meat.

1 apple, peeled and grated
¼ teaspoon salt
1 onion, finely diced
zest and juice of 1 orange
100 g caster sugar
½ teaspoon ground cinnamon
½ teaspoon ground nutmeg

2 cm piece fresh ginger, peeled and
    grated (about 1 teaspoon grated)
1 cup white wine
2 small pears, peeled and diced
50 g sultanas
½–1 tablespoon red wine vinegar

Method
Put the apple, salt, onion, orange zest and juice, spices, ginger and wine in a heavy-based saucepan. Bring to the boil and turn down the heat. Simmer about 30 minutes until the liquid has evaporated.
    Add pears and sultanas and bring back to the boil. Stir well. Add the vinegar and stir through and leave to cool. Keep refrigerated for up to 1 week.

Tip: Serve cold with Summit-smoked Wild Pork (see page 178).
    Makes about 2 cups

ROAST GARLIC AÏOLI

Roasting garlic gives it a sweeter, gentler flavour than using it any other way. Garlic also helps ward off any colds you might catch up in the highland winter.

1 head garlic
3 egg yolks
1 teaspoon wholegrain mustard
300 ml oil such as olive oil, canola or
    sunflower oil

2 tablespoons white wine vinegar or
    lemon juice
salt

Method
To roast a whole head of garlic, slice off the top of the garlic head to expose the cloves. Rub with oil, wrap in aluminium foil and roast at 180°C for about 45 minutes until very soft.

Squeeze each clove to remove soft garlic pulp. Place the garlic pulp, egg yolks and mustard in the bowl of a small food processor. Process until combined. With the motor purring, very slowly drizzle in the oil through the feed tube. As the mixture begins to thicken, add some vinegar or lemon juice.

Season with salt and more vinegar or lemon juice, as required.

Tip: Roast the garlic ahead of time and keep in a jar in the fridge covered in olive oil until needed.

The leftover egg whites will freeze well and can then be kept for at least 6 months.
Makes 1¼ cups

CAESAR SALAD DRESSING

1 egg
1 teaspoon sea salt
½ teaspoon freshly ground black pepper
1 clove garlic, crushed

1 teaspoon Dijon mustard
1 teaspoon lemon juice
2 tablespoons red wine vinegar
½ cup extra-virgin olive oil

Method
Place all ingredients in a screw-top jar, shake well and set aside.

SPEIGHT'S MUSTARD

This mustard is great with ham, beef or plain old sausages.

1 cup yellow mustard seeds
1⅓ cups black mustard seeds
1⅓ cups malt vinegar
1 x 330 ml bottle Speight's Gold
   Medal Ale
2 tablespoons caster sugar

1 teaspoon salt
pinch turmeric
3 cloves garlic, crushed
3 tablespoons olive oil
¼ cup water (more or less)

Method
Soak seeds in the vinegar and beer overnight in a glass bowl. (The seeds should absorb all of the liquid.)

Put the seed mixture in a food processor and process a bit to combine. You might need to do this in a couple of batches. Transfer mixture to a clean bowl.

Put sugar, salt, turmeric and garlic in the food processor with 4 tablespoons of seed mix. Blend well, before adding the rest of the seed mixture.

With the food processor running, drizzle the oil down the feed tube. Then, drizzle in just enough water to give the mustard a creamy consistency.

Spoon into clean jars and leave in a cool, dark place for four weeks before using.

Makes 4 medium-sized jars

TOMATO AND CORIANDER SALSA

This is the perfect accompaniment to corn fritters. It also makes a great dip.

500 g or 3 large ripe tomatoes, finely
   diced, seeds removed if wished
½ small red onion, finely diced
1 clove garlic, crushed
½ tablespoon chopped coriander

½ tablespoon chopped chives
2 tablespoons lime juice (more or less)
1 tablespoon olive oil
½ tablespoon brown sugar
salt and freshly ground black pepper

Method
In a bowl combine all the ingredients and adjust seasoning to taste, adding more lime juice if wished.

Makes 2 cups

LIME AND CHILLI DRESSING

This dressing is perfect with salmon or over a chicken salad or in coleslaw.

1 egg
½ teaspoon white vinegar
1 teaspoon runny honey
¼ cup sweet chilli sauce

¼ cup lime juice
15 g coriander leaves
250 ml light oil, such as sunflower
    or canola

Method
Place the egg, vinegar, honey, sweet chilli sauce, lime juice and coriander in a blender and mix. With the motor running very slowly pour in the oil until it is all incorporated and the dressing is thick. Store in the fridge for up to 5 days.
    Makes 400 ml

BALSAMIC DRESSING

Whip up this dressing, tip it over some rabbit food and you're bound to impress with your salad-making skills. But first, you'll need to find a clean screw-top jar to make it in, preferably one that isn't being used to store galvanised nails.

¼ cup balsamic vinegar
½ tablespoon honey
1 teaspoon wholegrain mustard
½ teaspoon salt

¼ teaspoon freshly ground
    black pepper
¾ cup extra-virgin olive oil
3–4 cloves garlic, crushed (optional)

Method
Place vinegar, honey, mustard, salt, pepper, olive oil and garlic, if using, into a clean screw-top jar. Shake well and season to taste with extra salt and freshly ground black pepper.
    If adding crushed garlic, keep dressing in the refrigerator.
    Makes 1 small cup

SMOKED TOMATO DRESSING

Who knew you could smoke vegetables as well as meat?
This is a smoky summer dressing, good for hearty salads.

Smoking parcel
handful of manuka chips
1 bay leaf
1 sprig of thyme or rosemary

2 medium tomatoes

Dressing
1 teaspoon wholegrain mustard
1 teaspoon Dijon mustard
2 teaspoons cider vinegar
½ teaspoon salt
150 ml light flavoured oil

Method
Preheat the oven to 200°C.
   Take a large square of tinfoil and place the smoking ingredients in the centre.
Seal by folding the edges tightly. Using a knife, poke 6 small holes in the top of the
parcel. Place the parcel in a roasting dish, place the tomatoes on top and cover the
whole thing tightly with tinfoil.
   Place in the oven and roast for 45 minutes until the tomatoes are soft and
smoky. Cool.
   Place the tomatoes in a blender with the mustards, vinegar and salt and blend to a
purée. With the motor running slowly drizzle in the oil. Keeps for 4 days in the fridge.
   Makes 2½ cups

BLUFF TARTARE SAUCE

This should be called tart-up sauce – it'll make your
fish 'n' chips seem really flash!

1 cup store-bought mayonnaise
1 teaspoon very finely chopped shallot
1–2 large gherkins, finely chopped

1 tablespoon capers, rinsed and chopped
1 tablespoon chopped parsley
juice of 1 lemon

Method
Put mayonnaise into a bowl and mix in the shallot, gherkins, capers and parsley.
Add lemon juice to taste.
   Makes 1 cup

BUTTERMILK BATTER

Using buttermilk makes a light, delicious batter.

50 g self-raising flour   200 g buttermilk
salt and freshly ground black pepper

Method
Place flour and seasoning in a bowl, then whisk in the buttermilk.

BUTTERMILK BATTER FOR ONION RINGS

Simply add the following seasoning to the basic buttermilk

batter and beat away.

3 teaspoons bittersweet smoked paprika   1 teaspoon garlic salt
1 teaspoon ground cumin

GENERAL INDEX

RECIPE INDEX

THANKS

We can't go without saying 'Good On Ya, Mate' to those
who have helped pull this book together:

All the Ale House owners and staff

Don Gordon, Speight's Brewery Historian

John Craig

Chris Snow

Sean O'Donnell

Mat Tolhurst

Lion Nathan

Nic McCloy

Aaron McLean

Fiona Smith

Kathy Paterson

Tam West

Gary Stewart

Marolyn Krasner

Publicis Mojo

3 Bald Men

the PR shop

Patearoa Road, near Waipiata

IT'S TIMES LIKE THIS YOU APPRECIATE YOUR OWN PLACE IN THE INTERNALLY ASPIRING COSMOS, BOY.

GOOD ON YA, MATE.